◆FOCUS◆
Reading for Success

Wheels and Rockets

PROGRAM AUTHORS
Richard L. Allington
Ronald L. Cramer
Patricia M. Cunningham
G. Yvonne Pérez
Constance Frazier Robinson
Robert J. Tierney

PROGRAM CONSULTANTS
Bernadine J. Bolden
Ann Hall
Sylvia M. Lee
Dolores Perez
Jo Ann Wong

CRITIC READERS
Mabel L. Murray
Marcia Savage

John C. Manning, *Instructional Consultant*

SCOTT, FORESMAN AND COMPANY
Editorial Offices: Glenview, Illinois

Regional Offices: Sunnyvale, California •
Tucker, Georgia • Glenview, Illinois •
Oakland, New Jersey • Dallas, Texas

ACKNOWLEDGMENTS

Text

Page 32: Adapted from "Green Salads and Love to a Sea Giant" by Opal Dean Young, *Wee Wisdom Magazine*, June/July 1981. Copyright © 1981 by Unity School of Christianity. Reprinted by permission of the author.

Page 53: From *Is Somewhere Always Far Away?* by Leland B. Jacobs. Copyright © 1967 by Leland B. Jacobs. Reprinted by permission of Holt, Rinehart and Winston, Publishers.

Page 56: Adapted from *Herbert's Treasure* by Alice Low. Copyright © 1971 by Alice Low. Reprinted by permission of the author.

Page 68: Adaptation of "Cross-Country" by Ellen Weiss from *The Electric Company Magazine,* December 1981/January 1982. Copyright © 1981 Children's Television Workshop. Reprinted by permission.

Page 80: "A Short Story" from *The Tightwad's Curse and Other Pleasantly Chilling Stories* by Margret Rettich. Translated from the German by Elizabeth D. Crawford. Copyright © 1978 by Annette Betz Verlag. English translation Copyright © 1979 by William Morrow and Company, Inc. Adapted by permission of William Morrow & Company.

Page 106: Adaptation of "The Strange Habit of Barney Brewster's Rooster" by Frances B. Watts, *Golden Magazine for Boys and Girls,* September 1966. Reprinted by permission of the author.

Page 132: Adapted by permission of Four Winds Press, a division of Scholastic Inc. from *The Big Orange Splot* by Daniel Manus Pinkwater. Copyright © 1977 by Daniel Manus Pinkwater.

Acknowledgments continued on page 479.

ISBN 0-673-72657-6
1991 printing
Copyright © 1988, 1985

Scott, Foresman and Company, A Division of Harper Collins *Publishers.* Glenview, Illinois. All Rights Reserved. Printed in the United States of America.

45678-RRC-9594

Contents

14

Animals—Take Care!

DINOSAUR BONES

Do you know what these people are doing? They are taking off the dinosaur's head. The dinosaur in this museum has the wrong head.

For years the people who put together dinosaur bones thought they had the right head on the right body. Now they have found out they made a mistake. So in museums all around the world, they are taking the wrong heads off dinosaurs and putting on the right ones.

People aren't always sure of the right way to put dinosaur bones together. There aren't any living dinosaurs around to look at.

Why the Dinosaurs Disappeared

What ever happened to the dinosaurs? Many scientists are looking for an answer to this question.

Some scientists think the dinosaurs died out because the weather changed. These animals needed warm air and sun to live. The earth became colder many, many years ago. This made the animals die.

Other scientists think the dinosaurs died out because there was a change in plant life. Many of these animals ate plants. If the plants died out, there would be no food for the plant-eating animals. They would die. Other dinosaurs ate meat. They ate other animals. If the plant-eating animals died, the meat-eating animals would have no food. They would die too.

A few scientists have other ideas. They think these animals did not all die out. They say there are places on the earth, like swamps, where a dinosaur could eat and sleep without being found. They think some of these animals are still living today.

Sharpen Your Skills

Details are small pieces of information. They may help you understand a selection, remember it better, or enjoy it more.
1. In the second paragraph on page 18, what details help you understand how a change in weather may have killed the dinosaurs?
2. On page 19, what detail tells why some scientists think dinosaurs are still alive?

Look for the details in "Danger in the Swamp" that help make the story fun to read.

Danger in the Swamp

by Samantha Reed

What if people really wanted to find a living dinosaur on the earth? Where would they go? What might they find? This story did not really happen, but it tells what their trip could be like.

"The weather is too hot" was my first thought when I reached this swamp in Africa.

I had come to Africa with Professor Ross Davis and three other scientists. I was a writer looking for a story. Professor Davis was looking for a live dinosaur. That sounded like a good story to me. Some people thought Professor Davis would never find a live dinosaur. Others thought he might. If he did, I wanted to be there.

For four weeks we did not find anything like a dinosaur. We did find lots of danger.

Because the land was a swamp, we could not use a car. We walked. Every day we were deep in water. The water was hot and dirty.

We were not the only things in the water. The swamp was filled with snakes. At the end of the first week Dr. Morgan, a scientist, was bitten. By working fast, Professor Davis gave Dr. Morgan medicine before the snake's bite made him sick. The medicine saved his life.

The ground was too wet to sleep on. We had to carry hammocks. Every night we would tie our hammocks to two trees. One night Dr. Morgan's hammock came off one tree. He fell into the dirty water. We cleaned the mud off him for two hours.

The swamp was a terrible place. There were no other people. We were bitten by bugs all the time. We lost our snake medicine. The trip was more terrible than meeting a dinosaur ever could be.

By the fifth week everyone was tired and dirty. We felt terrible. We all wondered if Professor Davis was wrong. Maybe there wasn't a dinosaur in this part of Africa.

On Saturday night we reached dry land. Then we saw something beautiful! A lake was in front of us. We walked to its shore and set up camp for the night.

By nighttime everyone felt better. We were dry. The weather was cooler. The bugs had disappeared. We weren't being bitten.

Suddenly I heard a splash. Rings of water were washing up on shore.

"Look!" Professor Davis yelled. "Out there in the lake!"

A long, dark "thing" rose out of the water. Slowly, very slowly, it began moving closer to shore.

Then, right in front of us, a head shot out of the water. It was dark gray and looked like a snake's head. Only it was the size of an elephant's. Its skin had no hair but was covered with bumps. Its terrible eyes glowed in the setting sun.

Davis said to us, "Walk away from the lake very slowly."

The animal followed us as we moved away from the lake. Once its head dropped down. It almost touched Dr. Morgan.

When we reached the swamp, the animal turned back. After we had walked for about an hour, I asked Professor Davis a few questions.

"Well, do you think you found your dinosaur?" I asked him.

"I think so," he said. "I'll know when I get a better look at it."

"A better look? When?" I asked.

"On the next trip." He smiled and looked behind him. "Oh, I'll be back. That animal and I are going to get to know each other!"

Checking Comprehension and Skills

1. Why did the writer go with Professor Davis and the scientists? (20)
●2. What details helped you know about the problems they had on this trip? (20-21)
●3. What details told you what the animal looked like? (22)
4. Did Davis find what he was looking for? Why do you think as you do?
5. Professor Davis said he'd be back. What do you think might happen on his next trip?

Which word would you use in each sentence?
glowed   fifth   earth
○6. We saw the animal during the ___ week of our trip.
○7. The animal's eyes ___ in a terrible way.

● Details   ○ Context and Consonants

Some Animals Didn't Disappear

Find the living animal on the left that is like the one in the rock on the right.

Disappearing

Animals

What would the earth be like without any animals? Many kinds of animals on earth are in danger. They might die out. No one wants animal life to disappear. That is why many people are working hard to save these animals. They don't want any kinds of animals to disappear.

Using Sense and Consonants

Baby seals swim in **c_ld** water.

What word goes next to the end of the sentence above? Can you think of a word that makes sense? Try one of these words:
called   deep   cold

Sharpen Your Skills

Both *deep* and *cold* make sense in the sentence. But only *cold* has the same consonants as **c_ld.**

- When you come to a word you don't know, think of a word that makes sense in the sentence.
- Then see if the consonants in your word are the same as the consonants in the new word.
- Be sure that *all* the consonants are the same.

What words go in these sentences?

1. I like to pr_t_nd that I am a seal.
   pretend   printed   play
2. Seals are dr_pp_ng wet most of the time.
   dropping   dripping   very

Did you pick *pretend* and *dripping?* Now read the words in these sentences.

3. Seals have a thick <u>layer</u> of fat under their skin. This fat helps them keep warm.
4. In winter, some seals live <u>below</u> the ice. They come to holes in the ice to get air.
5. They swim to the <u>bottom</u> of the water to get warm.
6. Other seals spend large <u>amounts</u> of time on top of the ice.

Use sense and consonants to figure out new words as you read about people who help animals.

The Best Animal Helper

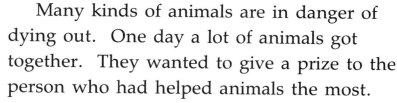

Many kinds of animals are in danger of dying out. One day a lot of animals got together. They wanted to give a prize to the person who had helped animals the most.

A sea lion stood up. It said, "I think the people who do the most for us are people who make good laws. Laws can protect animals."

Then an owl spoke up. "I think wildlife officials help animals the most. Officials make sure people do what the laws say should be done."

A wolf said, "I don't agree. Scientists are the people who help animals the most. They learn about us. They find out what hurts us. They learn what helps us. Then people can do the things that will help us."

Who should get the prize for helping the most? Should it be a person who makes laws? A wildlife official? A scientist? Someone else?

Finally a rabbit spoke up. "Many people help animals. We need the work of each of them. We can't give just one prize. Let's start an Animal Helpers Hall of Fame. All those who help us a lot can be in it."

The other animals thought this was a good idea. Are you helping animals? Perhaps you are in their Hall of Fame!

Sharpen Your Skills

When you read a story, try to sum it up—to tell what it is all about.
1. What did the animals want to do at the beginning of the story?
2. Which tells what the story is all about?
   a. Some animals decided a Hall of Fame would thank all people who help animals.
   b. Wildlife officials help animals a lot.

When you finish the next story, "Green Leaves and Love to a Sea Giant," try to sum it up.

Green Leaves and Love to a Sea Giant

by Opal Dean Young

My sister Elena and I were visiting our Uncle Juan in Florida. In the canal behind Uncle Juan's house, Elena thought she saw a huge "thing" under the water.

"Oh! It's probably just your shadow or a fish," I said looking over the side of the boat.

Suddenly I saw a dark brown nose on a huge, long, round, gray body. The body had short flippers. It had a wide tail shaped like a spoon. The huge animal quickly ate some lettuce that had dropped from my sandwich into the water.

"It's not your shadow! It's not any shadow! It's a sea giant!" I yelled. "Let's get out of here, Elena. Row!"

Elena turned the boat around. She began to row as fast as she could back up the canal. I kept watching the giant. It began to follow us! There it was, swimming right behind us!

I threw another little bunch of lettuce away from the boat. The huge animal ate it. Then it began to follow us again. We couldn't escape! If only Elena could row faster!

On up the canal we went. "Help us escape!" we began to yell. "Help us escape from this sea giant!"

But the giant did not stop. It just followed us up the canal, past many tall trees.

Up ahead, Mr. Mendoza was out in his garden watering his lettuce and other plants.

"Please, save us, Mr. Mendoza!" we called, when we had rowed up close. "Won't you help us escape from this sea giant?"

Mr. Mendoza turned and looked. He splashed water all over us and the giant.

That did not help. Elena rowed on around a bend in the canal.

Soon, a lot of people heard our yells. They came running along the canal, trying to help us. But the terrible animal kept following us!

After a while we came to Uncle Juan's boat dock. Uncle Juan was standing there, holding a big bunch of green plants.

"Save us, Uncle Juan!" I yelled.

The huge sea giant turned away from our boat when Uncle Juan began throwing bunches of green plants into the water. It slowly moved over to the dock with its flippers. It ate the plants.

"It's all right," said Uncle Juan, as Elena rowed to the dock. "It's only a sea cow. They live in some warm waters of Florida."

"A sea cow?" I asked, when Uncle Juan helped us to get out of the boat and on the dock.

"That's right," he said. "And a very hungry one, at that."

"Hungry?" My sister jumped back.

Uncle Juan laughed. "Don't worry," he said. "A sea cow eats only green plants."

I told Uncle Juan about the lettuce I'd dropped. I said the sea cow had eaten it.

"That's why it followed you," he smiled.

"But why did it look for food in the canal?" I asked. "Aren't there a lot of green plants for sea cows to find in the river where this canal begins?"

"There used to be," Uncle Juan explained. "But the plants are killed when people pollute the water by throwing all kinds of trash into it." He rubbed the sea cow's head.

Then I saw marks from deep cuts on the sea cow's back and flippers. "Look at those," I said.

Be kind to sea cows.
Don't poke or hit them.
Don't pollute by
throwing trash into
the canal.
SPEEDBOATS
SLOW DOWN !

"Sea cows move very slowly through water. They are often run over and cut by speedboats," Uncle Juan explained. "Other cuts on their bodies are made by people who hit them with things and poke them with sticks."

"How terrible!" my sister cried. "People shouldn't do that to them! They shouldn't pollute the water either."

Elena and I looked at each other. Then we knew that we had a big job to do.

That very afternoon, we made signs. People who lived beside the canal said we could put them up.

Uncle Juan smiled when he saw the signs. He said, "It looks like the sea cows will come up our canal often."

And they do! Now when my sister and I visit Uncle Juan in Florida, we always pick bunches of green plants—for our friends, the sea cows.

Checking Comprehension and Skills

1. How did Elena and her sister feel about the sea giant at the beginning of the story? Why did they feel that way?
2. How did the two girls feel about the sea giant at the end of the story?
3. What did the girls find out about sea cows that helped change their minds? (35-36)
4. What did they do to help the sea cows? (36)
•5. What is this story all about?
   a. The girls learned more about sea cows and decided to help the sea cows.
   b. The girls were visiting Uncle Juan.
   c. People are afraid of sea cows.
6. Have you ever tried to help a wild animal? If so, what did you do?

Choose the word that best finishes each sentence below.

camel   pollute   shadow
canal   present   speedboat

○7. Elena began to row the boat up the ____.
○8. Don't ____ by leaving trash around.

• Story Elements: Main idea
○ Context and Consonants

There are many ways of helping animals. Wildlife officials and people who make laws are helping animals in different ways.

There is one place where people help wild animals in another way. They work hard to keep the animals well. They show these wild animals to many people. The place where they work is the zoo.

Zoo doctor

Zoo keeper

Working at the Zoo

A good zoo is a place where the animals are kept healthy. It is not easy to keep a lot of wild animals healthy. It takes hard work and good care. Many people work at different jobs so the animals will stay well.

What if one of the animals does get sick? Who helps when a camel has a sore neck? Who gets called if a lion needs a tooth pulled? The zoo doctor, of course. These doctors treat all the sick animals. They treat elephants that have ear trouble. They set broken legs and wings. Many of the problems they treat are like the ones that people have. But others are very different.

The most important people in the everyday life of the animals are the zoo keepers. They feed the animals on time. They give them enough water to drink. They clean the cages. They exercise the larger animals.

Zoo director

Who decides which keeper takes care of which animal? That's the job of the zoo director. Most directors have worked with animals for years. They know both the animals and the workers. Directors make sure the zoo is a safe, healthy place for animals to live.

Sharpen Your Skills

The sentence that tells the main idea may be at the beginning, middle, or end of a paragraph.
1. What is the second paragraph on page 40 about—camels and lions or zoo doctors?
2. Which sentence in the paragraph tells the main idea?

Remember to look for the main ideas when you read the next two articles.

ZOO TEACHER

by Sheila Dawson

For two days a week, Donna Brookins is a zoo teacher. She tells people who visit the zoo about animals. Donna likes talking to people. She also likes working with the animals. So she is glad she can help the zoo by being a teacher.

To be a good teacher, Donna has to know many things about animals. The zoo trained Donna for more than three months before she began to teach.

When Donna talks to people who come to the zoo, she tells them everything she knows about an animal. Today she is showing a healthy, white ferret to a group of children. The ferret's name is Prince.

"Look how Prince moves in my arm," she says. "A ferret lives in holes under the ground.

Its backbone is not stiff. That helps the ferret move back and forth to get through the holes.

"A ferret's teeth are sharp. When you pet Prince, be sure to pet him near his tail. He may bite if you touch his head.

"Smell your hands after you have petted him. They may smell strange to you. The odor that he left is called musk. Ferrets leave that odor on anything they think is theirs."

When Donna puts Prince in his cage, she has the same odor on her skin. She does not care. She feels lucky to be able to hold a ferret.

Not many people ever get to hold a ferret. Ferrets are disappearing from the earth. There are fewer than one hundred wild ferrets left in the United States today. If people want to see ferrets, they probably can see them only in zoos.

"Zoos mean different things to different people," Donna says. "Some people think zoos are great places to have fun. Some people think zoos teach people about animals. But I like zoos because they save animals, like ferrets, that might die out. When I work here, I feel I'm helping to save animals too."

BABE SEES THE DENTIST

by Sue Massey

Zoo keepers at the Brookfield Zoo near Chicago were worried. They were worried because it had happened again. Babe the elephant was getting thinner and thinner. She was now only 5,660 pounds.[1] That may seem like a lot, but it wasn't for Babe. She had already lost 500 pounds[2] in three months.

Zoo doctors knew Babe wasn't healthy. They had looked in her mouth. They had found out that one of her four large teeth was crooked. The crooked tooth made it hard for Babe to chew her food. The doctors knew what had to be done. Babe had to have that tooth pulled.

Where do you find a dentist who pulls elephant teeth? The director of Brookfield Zoo found one in California. His name is Dr. Dave Fagan. Dr. Fagan had worked on three other elephants before he worked on Babe. He flew to Chicago from California for Babe's important operation.

---

1. 2,567 kilograms   2. 227 kilograms

The operation took three hours. About twenty zoo keepers and zoo doctors from Brookfield Zoo helped. Babe was put to sleep so she wouldn't feel anything. The doctors gave her oxygen through her trunk.

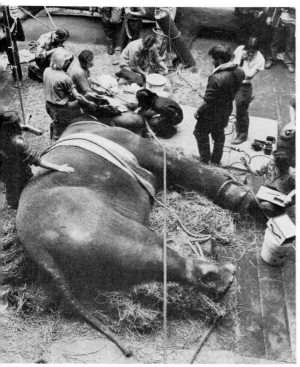

Oxygen goes into Babe's trunk from the oxygen tank.

Dr. Fagan has come from California. The operation is about to begin. First, Babe is put to sleep.

A big drill is used on Babe's tooth.

The tooth Dr. Fagan needed to pull was huge. It was 9½ inches[1] long. It was hard to pull. Dr. Fagan had to use a hammer and a crowbar. He even used a big drill.

1. 24 centimeters

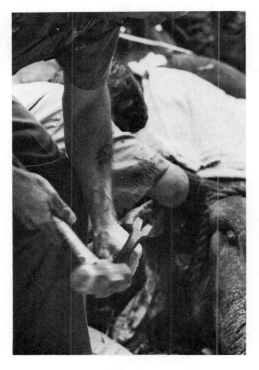

Dr. Fagan will have to pull the tooth out with a crowbar. He uses a hammer to get the crowbar into the hole that was drilled.

Dr. Fagan pulls hard on the crowbar.

Finally the important operation was over. The tooth was out. When Babe woke up, her keepers used large ropes to help her stand up.

Dr. Fagan said that Babe's mouth would be sore for a while. She would have to eat soft food. Soon, however, she could begin to eat like an elephant again. It wouldn't be too long before she gained back her 500 pounds.[1]

1. 227 kilograms

Men and women from Chicago newspapers watch the operation. Later they will write stories about Babe and her tooth.

With one last pull, the tooth comes out!

A zoo keeper displays the tooth that gave Babe so much trouble.

Checking Comprehension and Skills

1. Who is Prince? Why is he special? (42-43)
2. Do you think Donna Brookins is a good teacher? Why do you think as you do?
●3. Read the last paragraph of "Zoo Teacher." Which sentence tells the main idea? (43)
4. How is Donna Brookins's work like Dr. Fagan's work in "Babe Sees the Dentist"?
●5. Read the first paragraph on page 45. Which sentence tells the main idea?
6. What was Babe's problem? How was it solved?
7. Would you like to do the kind of work that Dr. Fagan does? Or would you rather do Donna Brookins's kind of work? Why?

Which word would you use in each sentence?
○8. He has been to the zoo more than ___ times.
   teacher   twenty   however
○9. Donna ___ a ferret to some children.
   hundred   important   displays

● Main idea and supporting details
○ Consonants and Context

Use What You Know

Nancy read this in a story.

"Detective Amy went through the papers in the old desk. She was trying to ferret out the missing picture."

At first Nancy could not figure out what *ferret* meant. Then she remembered something she had read last week. "A ferret is a small animal that goes in and out of holes under the ground, looking for food. I guess *ferret* can also mean 'to look for something' the way a ferret looks for food."

Do you think Nancy was right? Why or why not?

Remembering facts you learned before can help you understand new stories. As you read a story, ask yourself what you already know that can help you.

Don't forget—use what you know as you read.

Finding Out

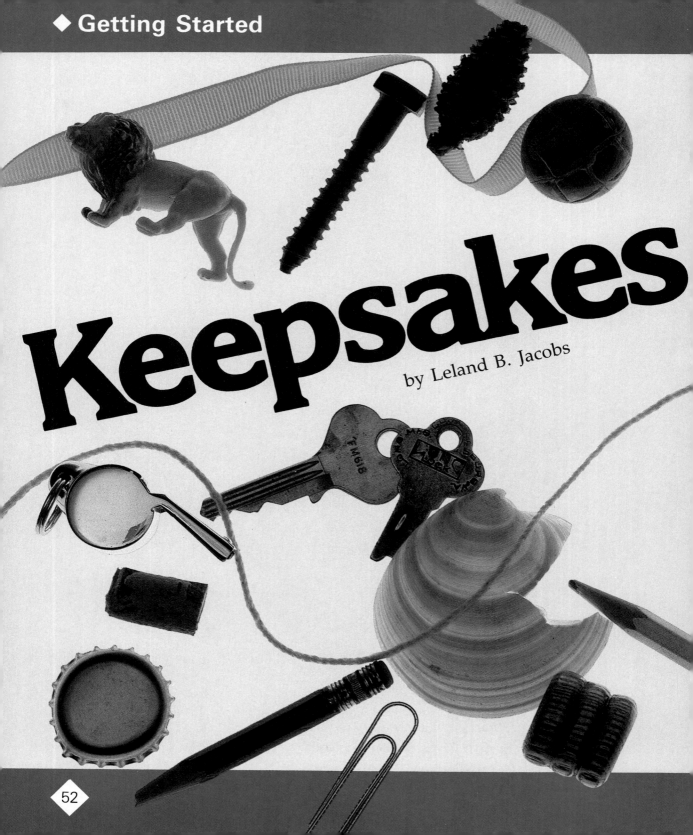

Keepsakes

by Leland B. Jacobs

I keep bottle caps,
I keep strings,
I keep keys and corks
And all such things.

When people say,
"What good are they?"
The answer's hard to get
For just how I will use them all
I don't know yet.

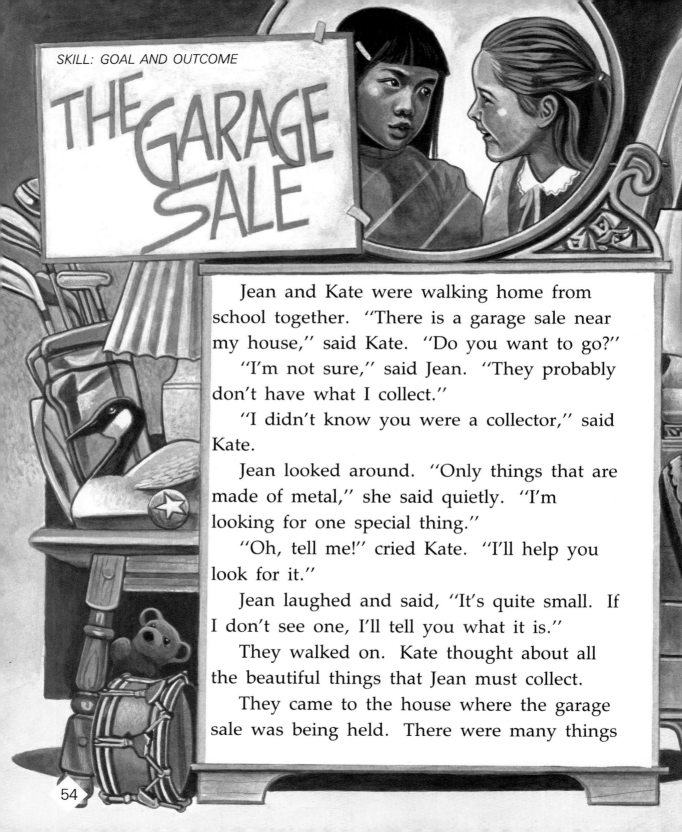

THE GARAGE SALE

Jean and Kate were walking home from school together. "There is a garage sale near my house," said Kate. "Do you want to go?"

"I'm not sure," said Jean. "They probably don't have what I collect."

"I didn't know you were a collector," said Kate.

Jean looked around. "Only things that are made of metal," she said quietly. "I'm looking for one special thing."

"Oh, tell me!" cried Kate. "I'll help you look for it."

Jean laughed and said, "It's quite small. If I don't see one, I'll tell you what it is."

They walked on. Kate thought about all the beautiful things that Jean must collect.

They came to the house where the garage sale was being held. There were many things

54

to look at. Kate saw that some were made of metal. There were little metal toys, screws, an old clock, and other metal things. "They must not be beautiful enough," Kate thought.

"What about the rings on this table?" she asked. "Do you collect them?"

"No," replied Jean. "It's so hard to find what you want when you are a real collector."

Kate wanted to help. But she did not know what Jean was looking for.

Just then Jean yelled, "There it is! The very thing I want!"

Kate could not believe her eyes. Jean had picked up an old bottle cap from a table.

Sharpen Your Skills

The characters in a story often want something. The story tells how the characters get what they want.
1. In this story, what did Jean want to find?
2. How did Jean get what she wanted? How did Kate want to try to help her?

Read the next story, "Herbert's Treasure," to see if Herbert gets what he wants.

Herbert's Treasure

by Alice Low

Herbert was a treasure collector. He liked everything about collecting treasures.

He liked getting up in the morning. He liked thinking about what he would find that day. He liked going to the town's old dump. He liked looking around. He liked bringing the treasures home and putting them in his room.

He liked looking at them too. Everywhere he looked in his room there was some kind of treasure—a hammer, a mirror, some screws, some corks for bottles, and pieces of glass. He just liked having treasures.

His mother and father didn't like it though. One day, his mother said, "Herbert, please. Herbert, throw something away!"

"I can't," Herbert said. "They are treasures."

"Junk!" his father said. "Nothing but junk!"

"You never know," Herbert said. "They might be useful—someday."

"This rusty can?" his father asked.

"I can keep things in it," Herbert said. He put three screws, four nails, and a doorbell in the can.

57

When his mother and father left, he dumped the things out of the can to look at them. The doorbell didn't work, but it might—someday. Most of all, he liked thinking about his treasures and what he could do with them—someday.

And so every afternoon, in rain or sun, Herbert went to the dump.

One day his father said, "Why do you go to that messy dump? We have a swing and everything just right for you."

"It's more fun in the dump," Herbert said.

The next day he brought back a broken shovel, a bent trumpet, a broken chair, and some table legs. And a real find—a lock. He put them on his toy shelves.

"Now look at your toys!" his mother said. "They are under all that junk. I mean it, Herbert, right now. Today! Please, Herbert, please throw something away."

"All right," Herbert said. He took everything off his toy shelves. He threw away some things. Then he put his treasures back on his toy shelves. He thought about the lock. It didn't work, but it might—someday.

It was fun to look around his room, but it was sad to go to the dump now because he had already taken almost everything from it. The only treasure left there was an old door.

He brought the door home on his wagon— slowly. He needed to think about where to put it. By the time he got to his room he knew.

But first he had to take the treasures out from under his bed. There was only one place to put them—on top of his bed. Finally, he pushed the door under his bed. That night Herbert slept on the floor.

The next morning Herbert's mother was very angry. She said, "This is it, Herbert. I mean it. *Today!* Herbert, *please,* Herbert, throw something away!"

"Don't worry. There's nothing more to find," said Herbert sadly, "unless maybe there's something *under* the ground."

He went to the dump with his shovel and began to dig. Mostly there were rocks. Then his shovel hit something hard that went *clang!* Metal! Only metal sounded that way.

He dug it up and took it home. There he washed it with the hose. It was a key!

It didn't fit the car door or the front door. But it had to open something. Nobody would make a key that didn't open anything.

He put it under his pillow and dreamed about it that night.

Maybe it was the key to a castle where he would be the king. Not a castle full of gold thrones and red rugs. It would be a castle with nothing in it—except his treasures. Nobody else would live there. It would be his own castle where no one could say, "Herbert, please. Herbert, throw something away!"

He could see it in his dream. And he could see himself coming in the door. The door was old and nobody else could open it because *he* had the key. He could see the lock too, rusty and old.

He woke up. The moon was shining on the rusty lock. He took the key from under his pillow. Slowly, he tried to put the key in the lock. It didn't fit. He turned the key over. The key still didn't fit. Not quite. He oiled the lock and tried to put the key in again. This time it fit! He turned it slowly. CLICK! The lock opened. The key fit the lock! It worked! He was very happy as he went back to sleep.

The next morning Herbert still felt happy when he woke up. And then he remembered why. It was going to be a busy day. He had a plan.

First he carried everything outdoors. His mother and father didn't ask what he was doing. They were just happy he was doing it—outdoors.

Herbert sawed and hammered for three days. Then he set in the doorframe and put on the door. He put the lock on the door. He opened the lock with his key, opened the door, and moved everything in.

Then he hammered some more and painted too. He made more shelves—shelves for his paint pots and the clock with no hands, his corks and screws and tools and pans. And for everything else.

Last of all, he moved himself in. It *was* a castle, just like the one in his dream. The floor and the windows were cracked, but there was room—room for his treasures and no one to say, "Herbert, please. Herbert, throw something away!"

The doorbell still doesn't work, but it might—someday.

Checking Comprehension and Skills

1. What did Herbert's parents think of his treasures? (56)
2. Do you think the things Herbert collected were junk or treasure? Why?
●3. What did Herbert want in the story? Why?
●4. How did Herbert get what he wanted? (62)
5. Do you think Herbert's story could happen in real life? Why or why not?
6. Tell what you think this saying means: "One person's treasure is another person's junk."

Which word would you use in each sentence?
○7. Not all treasure is money or ____.
   gold   home   hose
○8. Do you want to sit on the queen's ____?
   woke   throne   old

● Story Elements: Goal and outcome
○ Phonics: Vowels

Winter Changes

Winter is a time of change. The days are shorter. The nights are longer. Plants and animals change.

In many places, winter brings snow and ice. People have to wear warm clothes. Instead

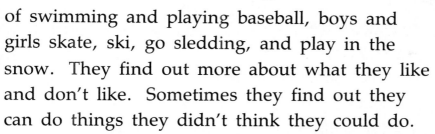

of swimming and playing baseball, boys and girls skate, ski, go sledding, and play in the snow. They find out more about what they like and don't like. Sometimes they find out they can do things they didn't think they could do.

Like summer, winter is a time of learning, finding out, and changing.

Gwen's Ice Skates

Norman enjoyed having his little cousin live nearby in Chicago. Gwen's family had just moved from California. It was January. When Norman was able to get away from college, he took Gwen different places.

One Friday night, Norman called Gwen on the phone. "Let's go ice skating tomorrow," he said. "I'll bring some skates your size."

"That sounds like fun!" said Gwen.

The next day, they went to a skating pond. Norman tried to teach Gwen how to ice skate.

"How can I stand on such thin blades?" Gwen laughed. "I've fallen down twenty times. I guess my ankles aren't strong enough."

"You'll get better. It just takes a lot of trying," said Norman. "Are you having fun?"

"Sure. It's fun anyway," answered Gwen.

The next Friday, Norman called Gwen again. "Would you like to ice skate again tomorrow?"

"OK," said Gwen. "But I think I could skate better if I wore my roller skates."

Norman started to laugh. "Who ever heard of wearing roller skates on ice? No roller skates! But there is a kind of ice skate for people who are learning. Each skate has two blades close together. I'll get a pair for you. I think you'll be able to stand better in them."

The next day, wearing the skates with two blades, Gwen did much better. Her ankles began to get stronger. It was easier to stand. And she only fell six times!

Sharpen Your Skills

The things that characters say and do help you understand their feelings and see what they are like.

1. What did Gwen say that shows she enjoyed learning to ice skate?
2. What are three things Norman did that show he liked Gwen?

Think about how Andrea and Michele act in the next story, "Cross-Country."

Cross-Country

by Ellen Weiss

Strong winds blew around the little
cabin. Michele finished putting wax on her
skis and looked out the window. The sky
was turning dark and gray.

"Andrea," she said to her big sister, "how can we go cross-country skiing? The radio said a blizzard will be here by night. We've only skied twice before. I can hardly stand on these things. What if I hurt myself?"

"Oh, don't worry so much," Andrea laughed. "We have at least three hours until night. Heavy snow won't come before then. Remember, you're with me, the best skier at my college. What can go wrong?"

"OK," said Michele. "I guess you know what you're doing."

They left the cabin and put on their skis. As they skied to the nearby woods, Michele thought, "Maybe this won't be so bad. Maybe the blizzard won't come today."

Everything had been fine so far. When their parents had decided they didn't want to go to the family cabin, Andrea had said that she would take Michele. Andrea was eight years older than Michele. The girls hadn't seen each other since Andrea had gone away to college. "It will give us some time together," she had said. "Don't worry. We'll be fine, just the two of us." So this weekend in January was theirs.

Michele stayed close behind Andrea as they went into the woods. It was much darker there than back by the cabin.

"Let's turn back," Michele said.

"Just a bit farther," said Andrea.

They kept going. Michele's toes were freezing. Her legs began to hurt. The skis felt too heavy to move. And she was getting angry at Andrea.

"There is a narrow bridge over a stream," Andrea called. "I'll ski across. You might want to take your skis off and walk."

"I might want to go back to the cabin," Michele said as she snapped off her skis.

Suddenly, Andrea screamed. Michele looked up to see what was wrong. Her sister was sitting in the middle of the bridge. She was in pain. Michele ran over to her.

"My ankle," Andrea groaned. "My ski must have hit a broken piece of wood on this bridge. I've hurt my ankle."

"Take the ski off and try to stand," Michele said.

When Andrea took the ski off, she tried to stand on her ankle. "Ow!" she cried in pain. "I must have sprained it badly."

"What are we going to do?" Michele asked. She saw what an awful spot they were in.

Andrea answered, "I can't even stand on my ankle. I surely can't walk on it in all this snow." She looked at her sister. "Michele, you're going to have to get us some help."

"But where will I go? How am I going to do it by myself? What if the blizzard comes?"

"You can do it," Andrea said. "Don't worry. Go to Slattery's Store over in Hancock. They have a snowmobile there. Mr. Slattery can come get me."

"But that's so far! It's going to get dark. The blizzard's sure to start! Why don't we just stay here and yell for help?"

"There's nobody to hear us," Andrea said.

Michele could see that Andrea was right. She would really have to go. "What if I get lost in the woods?" she thought. "Then we'll each be alone, and the blizzard will come."

"Now listen to me," Andrea said. "There's a narrow path through the woods. But it's not hard to follow. It comes out on the hill near Slattery's Store. Remember, keep the sun on your left. Then Hancock is ahead of you."

"OK," said Michele. "Here I go."

Michele set off on the path, feeling very alone. She looked back at the first bend. Andrea was swinging her arms to keep warm. Then Michele skied around the bend and couldn't see Andrea. She was by herself.

Michele pretended she was just out for a nice long walk in the woods in January. But she wasn't sure she was going the right way. Was she just going in big circles? "Keep the sun on your left," she thought.

She was really getting cold. "I can hardly feel my feet," she thought. "Andrea must be freezing back there all alone. She can't move around." Michele skied faster.

Soon Michele found herself at the top of a short, steep hill. At the bottom was a big stream—and another narrow bridge. She'd have to cross it! All by herself! Michele looked down from the top of the hill. She was afraid.

Michele took off her skis and walked slowly down the hill. By now, she wished she had never left the cabin. But she moved across the bridge, step by step. She had made it!

Michele climbed up the hill on the other side of the stream. She put her skis back on and pushed along. *Faster! Faster!* Now she felt sure she was going the wrong way. There was nothing to do, though, but to keep going. The sun was so low now that she wasn't sure she was even on the narrow path. The wind blew hard.

Suddenly the wind sounded a little different. The air felt different too. Michele took a few more steps and—she was out of the woods! She was standing at the top of a long hill. Michele looked down at the nearby lights of Hancock. She yelled with joy and skied down the hill slowly and carefully. Heavy snow had just begun to fall.

An hour later, Michele was warming her feet by Mr. and Mrs. Slattery's fire. She was drinking warm milk and listening to news about the blizzard on the radio.

"Mr. Slattery has been gone a long time with his snowmobile," she said to Mrs. Slattery. "Do you think he has found Andrea yet?"

"Don't you worry," Mrs. Slattery answered. "He'll find her, all right. You told him just which bridge she's stuck at."

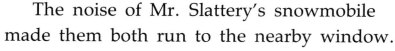

The noise of Mr. Slattery's snowmobile made them both run to the nearby window.

"She's safe!" yelled Michele.

Andrea hopped into the room. A small blanket was tied around her ankle. She began to cry when she saw her sister. "Oh, Michele, thanks. You're wonderful!"

Suddenly, the thought hit Michele. "Wow— I *was* kind of wonderful, wasn't I? I never thought I could do a thing like that by myself, but I did it. I really did it!" She smiled.

Then Andrea asked with a rush, "Are you OK, Michele? Was it awful? Did your feet freeze? Were you very scared?"

"I'm fine. It was all right." Michele hugged Andrea. "Don't worry so much!"

Checking Comprehension and Skills

1. When the girls set out skiing, why was Michele worried? (69)
2. Why did Andrea feel there wasn't anything to worry about? (69)
3. What did Michele have to do to get help?
- 4. How do you think Michele felt when she set off to get help?
- 5. How do you think Andrea felt when Michele left?
6. What is one thing that Michele did or thought about that helped her get to Hancock? (72-73)
- 7. Do you think that Michele was a very brave person? Why or why not?
8. How would you hope to act if you were ever in Andrea's place? In Michele's place?

Which word would you use in each sentence?
- ○ 9. She can't move because her ski is ____.
  stuck   sun   dark
- ○10. She was so excited she spoke in a ____.
  just   hurt   rush

- Story Elements: Character
- ○ Phonics: Vowels

People Get Lost

"Mark says he has lost his mother," said the girl to the woman. "He said she was right there with him and then she was gone. I asked him what she looks like. All he says is that she has on a brown coat and she looks like a mommy. This isn't going to be easy, is it?"

Vowels

How would you like to go to school in the year 2186? The picture shows who your teacher might be. See if you can read the words the teacher is showing on its screen. Remember that different letters can stand for the same vowel sound. Also, the same vowel letters can stand for different sounds.

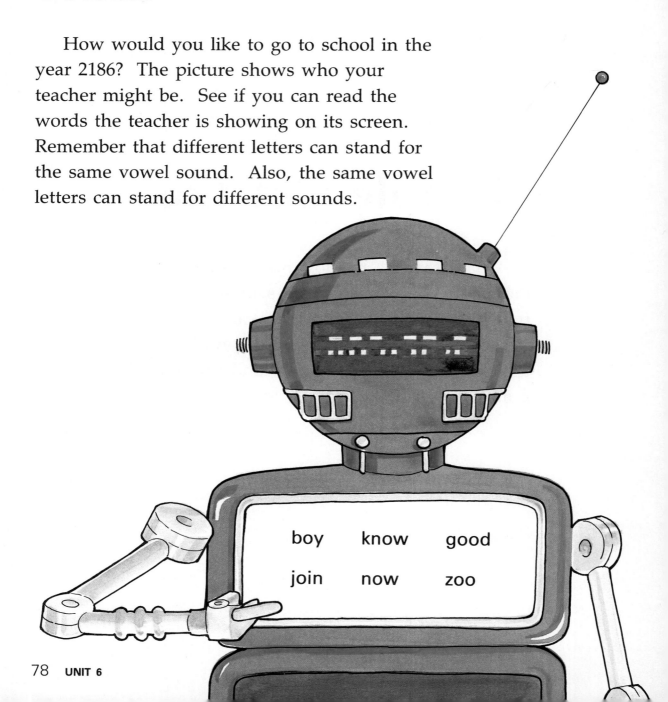

| boy | know | good |
| join | now | zoo |

Sharpen Your Skills

Look at the words from page 78 in the first box. Here's a rule to help you read such words:
- Different vowel letters can stand for the same vowel sound.

Read the four words in the next box. Here's a rule to help you figure out words like these:
- The same vowel letters can stand for different vowel sounds. You may have to try both sounds to figure out a word.

Use the vowel rules to help you read the underlined words.

boy
join

know
now
good
zoo

My Trip to 2186

1. It rained on May 1, 2186, so the ground was moist.
2. I have proof that I saw a school there.
3. People in 2186 wear wool pants.
4. Your frown tells me you don't think my story is true.
5. My trip scared me out of a year's growth. I may even be shorter now.

Try using the vowel rules on these pages when you need help figuring out words.

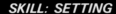

A Short Story

by Margret Rettich

One night a man stayed quite late at a nearby inn. When he finally left, it was pitch-dark outside. Nothing could be seen. He borrowed a walking stick from the keeper of the inn so he could feel his way home. The path he had to follow was dangerous because it went over a very, very narrow bridge.

Every time the man took a step, he felt in front of him with the stick. But after a short time, he tripped on a stone. He fell flat on his face. He hurt all over. When he got up again, the walking stick was missing. He felt around for a long time. Finally he got the handle in his hand. Then he started to go on.

He poked the stick to his left. Nothing.

He poked the stick to his right. Nothing there either.

"Oh," the man thought. "I'm already on the bridge." He poked in front of him so he wouldn't lose his way. But again his stick touched nothing.

"The bridge must have fallen!" he thought.

The man turned around quickly to go back. Again his stick touched nothing.

"Where am I?" the man wondered. He poked all around with the stick. Nothing!

He was so afraid that he stood without moving until it got light. Then he saw the inn beside him. The path was in front of him. The bridge was still ahead of him. He also saw that in his hand he held only the handle. The stick had broken off.

Sharpen Your Skills

Sometimes it is important to picture in your mind the setting of a story. The **setting** is where and when the story takes place.
1. Why is it important that this story takes place on a very dark night?
2. If the path had not gone over a bridge, how would the story have been different?

When you read the next story, "From Time to Time," decide when and where things happen.

From Time to Time
by Sue Alexander

Cast

GIRL   QT, a robot   GUIDE   DOCTOR
Four other guides   Four other people

Act 1

(Curtain rises. A room with a door but no windows. Table and chairs in the room look strange. In one corner, a robot. In center, on a low, narrow bed, is GIRL.)

GIRL *(Sits up slowly, rubs eyes, looks around.)*: What happened? Did I go to sleep? *(Walks around the room.)* Where is this place? These things are strange. This must be a table and chairs. *(Sits in one.)* It feels like a chair. Just doesn't look like one. *(Goes to robot nearby.)* What's this? A strange, metal vacuum-cleaner?

QT *(Hums, clicks, and rolls to her.)*: I am a vacuum cleaner, but I do much more than just vacuum. I am QT, a Class 1B working robot.

GIRL: Cutie! You don't look so cute to me.

QT: No, no! The letters *QT*. See! *(Points to letters QT on chest.)* I am here to work for you. Is there anything you want?

GIRL: I want to know where I am.

QT: Certainly. *(Touches wall. A map unrolls. Robot points to one spot.)* You are here.

GIRL *(chuckling)*: That's a good trick! Can you get me anything that way? Say, a fresh orange? *(QT touches wall. Orange slides out on dish.)* All right! No. Send it back. I don't want to eat. I want to look around. *(She starts to go to the door.)*

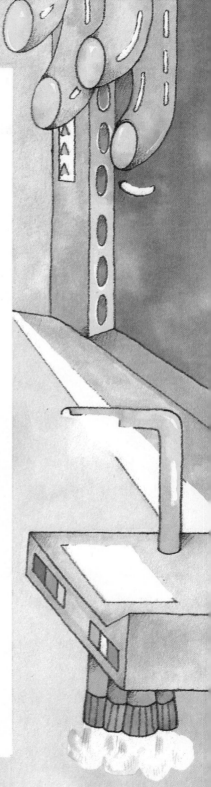

QT: No. You must wait here for a guide and the Doctor.

GIRL: What guide? What doctor? I don't want to see any doctor. I just want to go out. *(Reaches for the door handle.)*

QT: You must wait. Now try to stay quiet!

GIRL: No! No tin can named Cutie is going to keep me here if I don't want to stay!

QT: That is my job. *(Points at GIRL. A "zap" sound is heard. GIRL rubs eyes, lies down, and sleeps. QT goes to corner, chuckling.)* Tin can, one; girl, nothing. *(Curtain falls.)*

Act 2

(Curtain rises. GIRL *is waking up. She is watched by* QT, GUIDE, *and* DOCTOR. GUIDE *and* DOCTOR *are strangely dressed.)*

GUIDE *(helping* GIRL *up):* Please stand while the doctor looks at you.

GIRL: Am I sick? Are you going to make me stay in bed?

DOCTOR *(Moves a metal stick high above* GIRL.*):* Nothing like that. We just have to make sure you don't have any strange bugs that might make us sick.

GIRL: Where am I, then?

GUIDE *(Makes map unroll.):* You are here.

GIRL: I know I'm here, but where is here?

GUIDE: Newton, Ohio, the United States of America, Earth.

GIRL: Wait a minute! What's going on here?

QT *(chuckling):* She still doesn't know what's going on.

GIRL: Look! I live in Newton, Ohio, and there's no place like this in Newton, Ohio. People don't dress like you do. And there are no strange robots there. So, really, where am I?

DOCTOR: Maybe you should ask, "When am I?"

GIRL: When am I? It's about noon, isn't it? I was playing under a bridge—

GUIDE: The Green Street Bridge, right? You must have gone to just the right spot and slid through.

GIRL: Through what?

DOCTOR: Through time. You went under the bridge at noon on May 6, 1986. It's now about noon, May 6, 2186. You see, people do slide through now and again—

QT: From time to time. *(Pokes GIRL with its elbow, chuckling.)* Get it? From time to—

GIRL: I get it! I get it! Is this true?

GUIDE: You'll see for yourself. Since people from the past get here now and then—

QT: From time to time! *(Bends over laughing.)*

DOCTOR *(going to QT):* I'd better check you over. I think you've got a screw loose.

GUIDE: We welcome them here. We show the future to people like you. That is, we show them as much of the future as they can see from inside this building. Then we send them back to the same time they left.

GIRL: Why can't I go outside this building?

GUIDE: If something were to happen to you while you are here, the future would be different. But you can see a lot from inside. It's like one of your zoos. You and the animals can see each other. You just can't get together.

(Door opens. Four guides come in, all dressed the same. With them are four other people who have also slid through time.)

GUIDE: Are you ready to see the future?

GIRL: Ready! *(Pats QT on the head.)* I'll see you later, Cutie. *(Robot gives a low groan and goes to its corner. GUIDE, DOCTOR, and GIRL laugh. Curtain falls.)*

Checking Comprehension and Skills

•1. Where does the play take place? (82)

•2. When does the play take place? (86)

3. What are some things that QT could do?

4. Why was a doctor needed? (85)

5. Why couldn't the girl leave the building she found herself in? (87)

6. Do you think the girl was brave? Why?

7. Imagine going to any time and place you want. When and where would you go? Why? What do you think it would be like?

Which word would you use in each sentence?

○8. Let's have lunch together at about ___.
boy   room   noon

○9. The screw is ___ on that door handle.
now   loose   points

● Story Elements: Setting
○ Phonics: Vowels (variant sounds)

Make a Tin Can Robot

1. Get tin cans of different sizes that have nothing in them. Make sure the cans are clean. Make sure there are no sharp parts on the cans.

2. Decide what you want your robot to look like. Will it have a body and a head? Will it have arms or legs? Decide which cans would look the best.

3. Use tape and rubber bands to hold the cans together.

4. Get a marker—the kind with ink that will not wash off in water. Draw different parts on your tin can robot. You can draw buttons, eyes, a mouth, or anything you want.

Picture This!

Meet QT–2, a cousin of our friend QT the robot. QT–2 has a TV in its head. If you tell QT–2 any story, it can picture what happened in the story. What story is QT–2 picturing now?

Picturing stories is not hard to do. You can do it too. You don't even need a TV in your head. As you read, picture what the people in the story look like. How old are they? What clothes do they have on? What are they doing? Where are they? What does the place look like?

When you picture a story, you can understand it better. So be your own TV. As you read the other stories in this book, picture them!

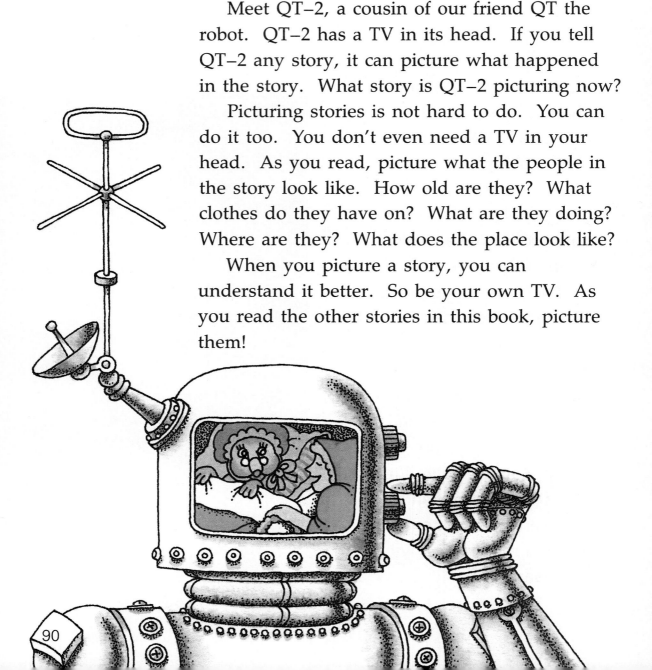

Section Three

From Here to There

3

BIKES

Slow—enjoying a ride with a friend

Fast—needing to get there in a hurry

Slow—pushing a broken bike

Fast—racing the wind just for fun

Slow—thinking about a problem

Fast—riding a ten-speed in high gear

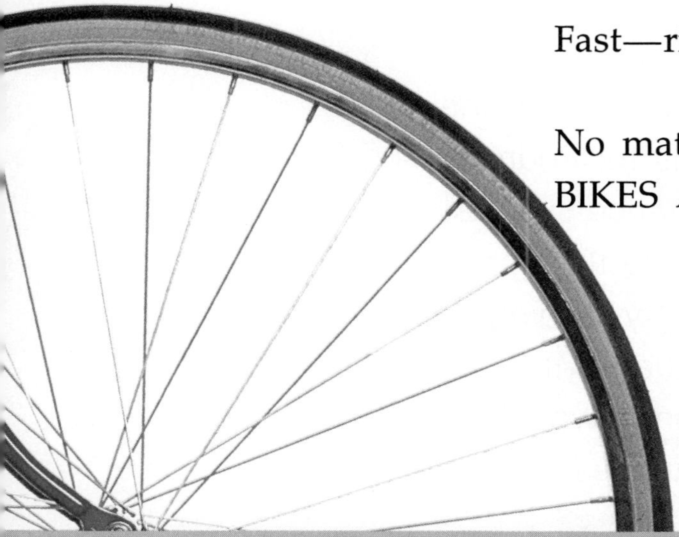

No matter what speed,
BIKES ARE FUN!

Words That Stand for Other Words

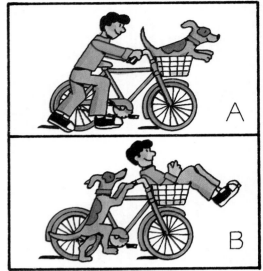

Pedro took his dog, Rex, home from the vet's office. <u>He</u> put <u>him</u> in the basket and walked the bike home.

Which picture shows what really happened? Who do you think walked the bike—Pedro or Rex? Who was in the basket? You probably decided that picture A is right.

Sharpen Your Skills

Often when you read, you will see that one word stands for another word or words. In the second sentence above, *he* stands for Pedro and *him* stands for Rex. If a sentence like that seems hard to understand, try these tips:

- Read the sentence again. Then try reading the sentences that come before and after it.
- Think about how the hard sentence would make sense with the other sentences.

Read the following story. Think about the underlined words and ask yourself who or what each word stands for.

Celia and Mom wanted to go to the zoo. They decided to ride their bikes because it was not very far to the zoo. In almost no time, Celia and Mom were there. Celia took Mom to the seals first. She liked to watch seals play, but Mom didn't like seals. Mom liked the lions better, but those can be dangerous animals.

1. Who rode the bikes?
2. Where were Celia and Mom in almost no time?

Reading the first four sentences again will help you answer the questions. The word *they* tells you that Celia and Mom rode the bikes. *There* tells you they were at the zoo in almost no time. Now try these:

3. Who liked to watch the seals play?
4. Which animals can be dangerous?

In the next story, think about what words like *they, those,* and *she* stand for.

One of a Kind

by Marianne
von Meerwall

There always seemed to be something wrong with Patricia Ann's bike. Sometimes a tire was flat. Sometimes the chain was broken. Sometimes the gears wouldn't work. Sometimes the seat was loose. There was always something different that needed fixing.

No matter what went wrong with the bike, Patricia Ann fixed it. If she didn't know how to fix it, she learned.

Once the bicycle had been beautiful and streamlined—a thing of joy to look at. People had gazed at it and talked about its beauty.

But the bike had gone through many years and many different owners. Now it just looked old. Patricia Ann didn't care. It was her bicycle, and she loved it.

One day, something terrible happened to the bike. Patricia Ann had parked her bike near the street and had gone inside her house. Later, a garbage truck backed up. The driver didn't see the bike, and the truck ran over it. SMASH!

Patricia Ann heard the noise. She was on the spot almost as soon as she heard it.

She stood gazing at her smashed bike. The truck driver got out and looked at the

smashed bike. They both felt terrible. The
bike looked as if it had turned its last wheel.
It looked as if it would have to be scrapped.

The truck driver wanted to help Patricia
Ann. He collected garbage. Sometimes, one
person's garbage can be another person's
treasure. So the truck driver began looking
for bike parts. As he found each one, he and
Patricia Ann would put it on the bicycle.

It took a while, but, when they were
finished, they had something they could really
be proud of. And they certainly had a bike
that was one of a kind. It was a thing of joy
to gaze at—again.

Bikes of the Future—
Streamlined and FAST!

by Marianne von Meerwall

For almost a hundred years, bicycles have looked about the way they do now. They have had two wheels of the same size. They have had handlebars, a seat, pedals, a chain, and gears. Since bicycles don't look special, what is so wonderful about them?

Bicycles are clean. They don't use gas to get you from one place to another. So they don't pollute the air like cars and trucks do.

Bicycles don't make noise. You can zoom down a hill on a bike. Or you can race across flat ground. About the only sound you will hear will be that of the wind in your ears.

Bicycles are good for you. They give you lots of exercise. They can make you feel great.

These are good reasons for riding bicycles. Then why are there so many cars on the road? Because you can get wet riding a bike. You can get cold. And bikes can't go as fast as cars can.

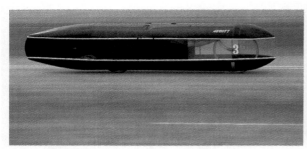

All of these things are true of bicycles of the past and the present. What about bicycles of the future?

The bikes of the future won't look like those of today. They will have a covering that will keep you dry and warm. Because of the streamlined covering, they will be able to go 40 to 50 miles[1] an hour. They will also be easier to pedal than today's bicycles.

These bicycles of the future are called human-powered vehicles, or HPVs. A vehicle is something that carries people or things. Human-powered means that a person makes the vehicle go. Your bike is a human-powered vehicle because *you* make it go. But usually only the special streamlined bicycles of the future are called HPVs.

---

1. 64 to 80 kilometers

For years people have been working to make better HPVs. Some of these people get together each year to race their HPVs. By trying new ideas, they almost always go faster than before.

The HPVs in the races must be *only* human-powered. They cannot use any gas. There must be no outside help.

Given this rule, people have built some really different vehicles. Some of the HPVs are pedaled by one rider. Some are pedaled by two riders. In some, the riders sit up. In others, the riders lie face down or on their backs. The streamlined coverings make some of the HPVs look very strange. They make others look very beautiful. Some of the HPVs have cost less than $50 to make. Others have cost over $3,000.

Many of these ideas will be used for HPVs that may soon be for sale. Someday you may ride one to school or to the store. It will be streamlined and FAST!

Checking Comprehension and Skills

1. What did Patricia Ann want to do about her smashed bike? How did she do it? (96-97)
2. What kind of a person was Patricia Ann? the truck driver?
3. Could what happened to Patricia Ann's bike have taken place with an HPV instead of a bike? Why?
4. What are some reasons why an HPV would be better than a bike? (99)
5. Might we be riding HPVs to school soon? Why do you think as you do?
6. Would you like to have an HPV? Why?
- 7. In the first paragraph on page 98, what does the word they stand for?
- 8. In the last paragraph on page 100, what does the word it stand for?

Which word would you use in each sentence?
○ 9. Some HPVs can carry two ___.
   riders   ride   riding
○10. A good bicycle ___ uses her hands to show which way she is going to turn.
   drive   driving   rider

- Referents
○ Structure: Root words with spelling changes

Crossing Busy Streets

How is this girl going to get across the street safely? She will do what you know you should do. She will wait until the traffic light turns green. Then, before she starts walking, she will look in both directions anyway. This way she will be sure that no cars or bicycles are coming or turning the corner.

My Son, the Policeman

Mrs. Kelly wondered about a new habit of her nine-year-old son Billy.

"He wants to be a traffic policeman," she would tell her friends.

"Oh, that's nice," her friends would say.

"He practices every day," Mrs. Kelly would say.

"*What?*" her friends would say.

Mrs. Kelly would explain. "My son Billy pretends the other children are cars. He makes arrows out of paper and tapes them to his hands. He points the arrows to tell the children where they may go in the house and how they may get there."

"Oh my," her friends would say while they shook their heads.

Things went on like this for almost a year. On Billy's tenth birthday, Mrs. Kelly baked her son a cake, which she shaped like a stop sign.

She hoped Billy would get the idea and stop practicing.

"Guess what, Mom," Billy said as he finished his last bite of cake. He pulled the arrows out of his back pocket and put them on the table. "I don't want to be a traffic policeman now."

"Oh, good," sighed Mrs. Kelly. "What have you decided to be instead?"

"A house painter," said Billy. "I've found some old paint. Now I'll go practice on the front of our house."

Sharpen Your Skills

Connecting words like *and, while,* and *which* often join two ideas together in one sentence.
1. What two things did Billy's arrows tell the children? What connecting word was used?
2. When Mrs. Kelly's friends learned what Billy did, they did two things at the same time. What did they do? What word told you this?

Read about a rooster crossing a busy highway in the next story. Notice how connecting words are used to put two ideas together.

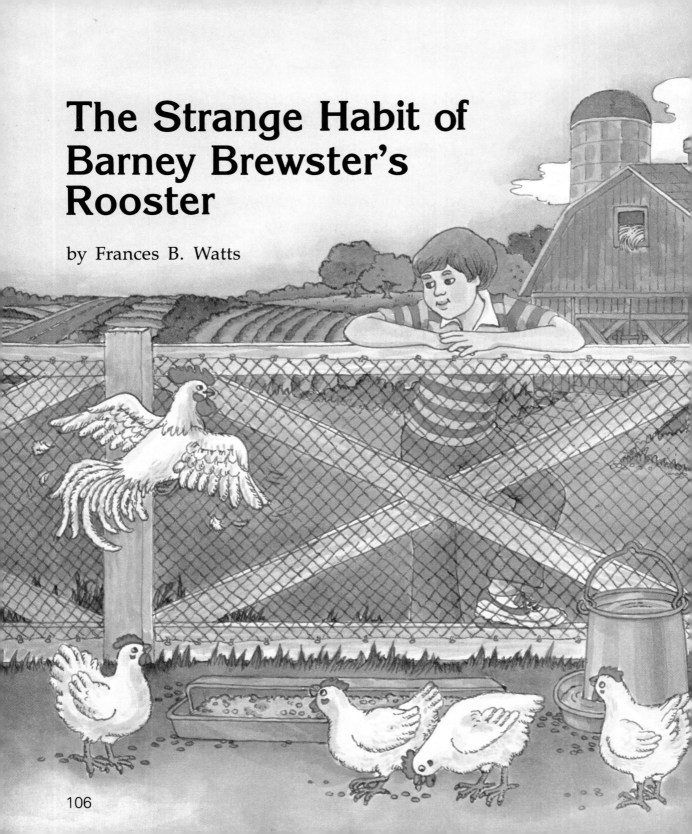

The Strange Habit of
Barney Brewster's
Rooster

by Frances B. Watts

Barney Brewster lived on a farm where there were hundreds of chickens. Barney's father locked them behind a fence. The Brewster farm faced a dangerous curve on a very busy highway. The traffic was the busiest around six o'clock. That is when the town pickle-packing plant closed for the night. Then pickle packers would zoom by, driving home to supper.

Most of the Brewster chickens were quite happy to stay behind the fence eating corn. But there was one rooster named Franklin who was different from the others. He kept flying over the fence to see what was happening.

Franklin began to follow Barney all over the farm. While the boy worked in the garden, Franklin tried pulling at the weeds with his bill. When Barney went fishing, the rooster sat and watched him. When Barney caught a fish, Franklin threw back his head and crowed.

Barney said to his parents, "That Franklin is one smart rooster. May I have him for my very own pet?"

"I can't see why not, if you take good care of him," Mr. Brewster replied.

For a long time Franklin stayed out of trouble. Then, the rooster began to do something very strange. He decided that he liked to go to bed on Mr. Garfinkle's gas pump. Mr. Garfinkle owned the gas station across the road. Every evening at six o'clock, Franklin would walk across the highway. He would sit on Mr. Garfinkle's gas pump. There he would sleep until the next day.

Franklin's strange habit caused Barney to worry. The rooster's bedtime was the same as closing time at the pickle-packing plant. He would cross the road just as the pickle packers came zooming around the curve. They never tried to slow down, though there was a sign on the road that said DANGEROUS CURVE. During the past year there had been seven crashes on the curve. They had been caused by speeding pickle-packers. But the pickle packers just would not learn to slow down. And here was Franklin, walking across to the gas pump while the traffic was the busiest.

Barney tried several different ways to break Franklin's habit. He tried talking to him about

UNLEADED REGUL

highway safety. He told him crossing the road was dangerous. Barney's talks did no good.

So the boy tried locking Franklin behind the fence just before the pickle packers drove by. But Franklin flew right over it. Once Barney tied the rooster to a tree. Franklin untied the rope with his bill and walked across the road to the gas station.

"I guess you can't teach a rooster safety rules," Barney said to his father.

That night, while the boy lay in bed, he tried to think of a plan. He remembered seeing signs on highways that said DEER CROSSING. Drivers slowed down because deer might cross the highway at that place. Barney decided that he would make a sign for Franklin which would solve the problem.

GARFINKLE'S GAS STATION

GARFINKLE'S GAS STATION

UNLEADED   REGULAR

$ 18.00 $ 11.00
TOTAL PRICE   TOTAL PRICE

0.07½   0.09½
GALLONS   GALLONS

The next morning Barney found a big wide board which he painted white. Then he painted big black letters on the board. They said ROOSTER CROSSING. He nailed the wide board to a thin board. Then he put the sign up the road from Mr. Garfinkle's gas station.

Just before six o'clock Barney sat by the road to see what would happen. Soon the first pickle-packer came zooming along. The driver slowed down when he saw the sign. He looked interested. He drove around the curve very slowly. Barney's idea had worked!

Soon another pickle-packer came along. It was Mr. Sudbury, a friend of Barney. Mr. Sudbury saw the boy. He stopped his car.

"Say, Barney, what does that sign mean back there?" he asked.

"Just what it says," Barney replied. "My rooster has a strange habit. Every night at six o'clock, Franklin walks across the highway to sleep on Mr. Garfinkle's gas pump. Drive more slowly. You might see him doing it."

Mr. Sudbury laughed. "Is that a fact?"

"Yes," said Barney. "Here comes Franklin now. Watch him."

Mr. Sudbury watched while Franklin marched across the Brewster yard. He saw him walk across the road. Then he watched Franklin fly up to the top of the gas pump and sit down.

Mr. Sudbury laughed and laughed. "Well, I've never seen a rooster do that before. But I can't disagree with my own eyes!" he said.

By this time, a line of cars had stopped behind Mr. Sudbury's car. The pickle packers got out of their cars to see what was happening.

"What is causing people to stop?" one asked.

Another one yelled, "What does ROOSTER CROSSING mean?"

Then Mr. Sudbury explained to them about the strange habit of Barney Brewster's rooster.

"Oh, I would like to see that rooster getting ready for bed!" one man spoke up. 'Tomorrow night at six o'clock, I'm going to slow down and watch for him."

ROOSTER CROSSING

After that evening, cars hardly ever speeded around the curve. The pickle packers talked about Franklin all over town. "Be sure to slow down at six o'clock by the sign that says ROOSTER CROSSING," they told their friends. "You might see a very unusual sight."

Barney Brewster was happy. Franklin was safe, and, what was even better, there were no more crashes on the dangerous curve. At the end of the year, the town gave Franklin a blue-and-gold ribbon for helping to make the highway a safer place to drive.

Barney was filled with pride. "Oh, my," he said to his parents. "If people can't teach roosters about traffic safety, roosters can teach people! That's what I think."

Checking Comprehension and Skills

1. Was the Brewster farm built in a dangerous place? Why do you think as you do? (107)
2. Who was Franklin? Why did Barney want him as a pet? (107)
3. Why did Barney worry about Franklin? (108)
4. Why did the pickle packers slow down for the sign Barney made?
5. What kind of a person do you think Barney was?
6. What would you have done to solve the problem of keeping Franklin safe?
- 7. Read the first sentence on page 110. What is the connecting word in the sentence?
- 8. Read the first sentence of the second paragraph on page 111. What is the connecting word in the sentence?

Which word would you use in each sentence?
- 9. He had a very ___ dream last night.
   safer   driver   unusual
- 10. She and I ___ about what we should do.
   disagree   slowly   packer

- Connecting words
- Structure: Prefixes and suffixes

LOUIS CROSSING

There goes Louis again!

Louis is a dog who likes to shop. He crosses the street every day to get food in a store.

Several years ago a car hit Louis. When he got well, people put up a sign. He still has his strange habit. But he is safer now.

The Strange, Amazing, Wonderful Gifts

a story from the Arabian Nights
retold by Lee Walker

In a land far away, in a time long before
this one, there lived a king. This king had
three sons. Prince Hussein was the oldest,
Prince Ali was the next, and Prince Ahmed
was the youngest. A little girl, Princess
Nuronnihar, also lived in the palace. She was
the child of the king's friend who had died.
The king cared for her as if she were his own.

As the four children grew up, they came
to love one another. When they were all old
enough, each of the three young men wanted
Princess Nuronnihar to be his wife.

Now the king and the princess thought it
fine that one of the princes would wed the
princess. But which one should they pick?

After much thought, the king called his sons to him. "My sons," he said, "you each love the princess, and she loves each of you. As she cannot decide which to wed, we'll have a contest. Each of you will go into a different country and find the most wonderful thing you can. At the end of a year, you must come home. The princess will wed the one who brings the strangest, most amazing, most wonderful gift." They all thought this was fair.

The next day, the three princes went off together. That night they camped on a hill. The next morning they promised to meet on the same hill in one year. Then each went off in a different direction.

Prince Hussein, the oldest, traveled north for many weeks. He came at last to a city in a country by the sea. There he went to the market and saw many wonderful things. There were lovely painted jars and fine white dishes.

But Prince Hussein was surprised to learn the price being asked for a certain plain carpet. "One hundred gold pieces!" he cried. "That is far too much for something so plain."

"There is nothing plain about this carpet," said the seller. "Anyone who sits on this carpet and wishes to be in another place will fly to that place in a moment. Try it."

So the seller and Prince Hussein both sat on the carpet. Prince Hussein wished to be across the city. And they were there!

Prince Hussein was glad to pay the hundred gold pieces. Surely his brothers would find nothing as wonderful as this flying carpet!

Prince Ali, the second son, had traveled a long way also. At last, he came to a city in a different land. He went into the market where he saw amazing things. There were silver bells, feathered fans, and the glow of gold on every side. Then he saw something different. It was long, but small around, and had glass at each end.

The seller said, "This sells for one hundred gold pieces because it is a magic glass. The one who looks through this glass can see anything he wishes to see. Try it."

So Prince Ali put the glass to his eye. He wished to see Princess Nuronnihar. And there she was, walking in the palace gardens!

Prince Ali was so pleased that he paid the hundred gold pieces. Surely his brothers would find nothing as amazing as this magic glass!

Prince Ahmed, the youngest son, had traveled even farther than his brothers. In a great city in a far country, he went into the busy market. Plants and fruits of every kind and color made the air sweet. He saw bright birds and strange animals.

No wonder, then, that he did not much care for a small apple made of wood. When he heard the price, he laughed, "A hundred gold pieces! That is far too much."

"Oh no, my friend," said the seller. "This apple is magic. Anyone who is sick has only to smell this apple to be made perfectly well."

To make sure, Prince Ahmed found a man who was very sick. He let the man smell the apple. And right away, the man became well!

Prince Ahmed was happy to pay the hundred gold pieces. For surely his brothers would find nothing as strange as this magic apple!

And so, one year from the time they had parted, the three young princes met on the hill. Each showed the others his wonderful gift and explained what it could do.

Just then, Prince Ali looked through his magic glass. "Why, the princess is very sick!" he cried. "She is going to die!"

"This apple can make her well!" cried Ahmed. "But how can we get there in time?"

"We'll fly on the carpet!" cried Hussein.

All three sat down on the carpet. All three wished very hard to be with the princess. In a moment, they were by her side. Prince Ahmed held the apple near her face. Up the princess jumped, as well as she could be.

When the king learned that his sons were home, he called them and the princess to him.

How happy they were to be together again. The king gave thanks that they had come home safely and that they had saved the princess.

Then the princes showed the king and the princess the gifts they had brought. They asked her to decide which young man she would wed. But she could not.

"Oh, my sons," said the king. "Each of these gifts is strange, amazing, and wonderful. The magic apple made the princess well. But without the magic glass, you would not have seen that she was sick. Without the flying carpet, you could not have come to her in time to save her life. It seems that no one of these things is more wonderful than the others. We will have to decide in another way whose wife the princess will be.

"Each of you will shoot an arrow into the air. The one whose arrow goes farthest will wed the princess."

So the princes got their bows and arrows. They got on their horses and rode out into a field. The king and others came to watch.

Prince Hussein, the oldest, shot his arrow first. His arrow went far indeed. Prince Ali shot next. His arrow went even farther. Prince Ahmed, the youngest, shot his arrow last. But, strange as it seems, Ahmed's arrow was lost. Everyone looked for a very long time, but Ahmed's arrow could not be found.

Now the king had to decide. He finally said, "Prince Ahmed's arrow probably went the farthest. But since it cannot be found, we do not know for sure. Prince Ali and Princess Nuronnihar will be wed." So it was decided.

People came from near and far to the wedding. There was a feast and dancing. The young prince and princess were very happy.

And what became of the oldest son? Prince Hussein felt so sad that he went to live by himself in the mountains.

And what became of the youngest son? Prince Ahmed kept on looking for his arrow. And do you know—? But that is another story.

Using a Dictionary

Lori has a problem. She has put all of the picture together except for the last piece. But that piece is missing! What can Lori do? Now she'll never know what the picture shows.

Suppose Lori had been reading instead. Suppose she had found the following sentence at the end of a story.

As a reward for helping the princess, the king gave the prince a large ruby.

If Lori didn't know what a ruby was, that sentence would be just like a picture with a missing piece. What could Lori do? First she could try to figure out a meaning that made sense in the sentence. Then she could look up the word in a dictionary.

123

Sharpen Your Skills

A **dictionary** is a book that lists words and their meanings. A **glossary** is a short dictionary you find at the back of some of your schoolbooks.

Words in a dictionary or glossary are listed in alphabetical order. Lori could find the page she needs quickly by checking the guide words. **Guide words** are the two words in large, dark print at the top of each page. They tell the first and last words explained on that page. The guide words on this page are *rooster* and *sea.*

500 **rooster | sea** ——— guide words

roost·er   a full-grown male chicken. See the picture.

ru·by   a clear, hard, red stone that is worth much money.

run   go by moving the legs quickly; go faster than walking.

rooster

rust·y   covered with rust; rusted.

sack   a large bag made of cloth.

sea   a large body of water: *The boat floated on the sea.*

entry word   definition

Lori could find *ruby* on this dictionary page because *ruby* comes between *rooster* and *sea* in alphabetical order. The words that are explained in a dictionary or glossary are called **entry words.** Can you find the entry word *ruby?*

An **entry** is an entry word and the information about it. A **definition** tells what an entry word means. What is the definition of *ruby?* Now Lori knows what the king gave the prince!

Some entry words have a picture to go with them. Which word on the dictionary page has a picture? For some words, there is a sentence in special print after the meaning. It shows how the word is used with that meaning. Can you find the sentence in special print for the word *sea?*

Now see if you can answer these questions.
1. Could the entry word *raccoon* be on the same page as *rooster* and *sea?* Why or why not?
2. Find the definition for *sack.* What is a sack made of?

Remember that a dictionary or glossary lists words and their meanings. Use a dictionary if you need to look up words as you read this book.

Books to Read

Bicycle Rider by Mary Scioscia

Young Marshall Taylor, his mother said, could ride a bicycle faster than any horse and buggy in Indiana. This true story tells how Marshall entered and won his first big bicycle race back in 1892. He went on to become the fastest bicycle rider in the world.

Dinosaurs and Their Relatives in Action by Tanner Ottley Gay

Where did the dinosaurs live? What kind of animals were they? How were their fossils formed? Find answers to these and other questions in this exciting book.

Let's Visit a Super Zoo by Georgeanne Irvine

At the San Diego Zoo, in southern California, you can see giant pandas, Sumatran tigers, and other rare animals almost as they live in the wild. If you can't get to San Diego, you can visit the zoo by reading this book.

A Thing of Beauty

127

PAINTINGS

Paintings mean different things to different people. People who paint and people who look at paintings do not always agree on what is beautiful or important or special.

Some people like paintings that show things the way they really are. Other people like paintings that show unusual shapes and colors. What kinds of paintings do you like?

After the Dance

Years ago, Beth Lorenzo was the star of a dance company. Her dancing was like a painting come to life. She loved to dance. And what she felt came through to people who saw her.

But then one night, Beth was in a bad car accident. Her right ankle was crushed.

In the morning, Beth woke up in the hospital. A doctor said, "Your ankle needed a lot of work. Now just rest and get well."

Beth quickly asked her most important question. "Will I be able to dance again?"

The doctor answered, "It's too early to say. It will depend on lots of things."

Beth felt sad after the doctor left. Life would seem empty if she could not dance.

Beth's worried brother tried to help her. Each day he took a different book, a record, or some pictures to Beth. Then one day he gave Beth a paintbrush.

As Beth painted her first picture, her spirits lifted. She poured out her feelings on the canvas just as she had poured them into her dancing.

Beth's ankle did not heal for a long time. When it did heal, she was never able to dance again. But her painting kept her happy.

As the years passed, Beth became better at painting. She began to show her paintings in art shows, and many people heard about her. They thought her paintings were like a beautiful, happy dance of colors.

Sharpen Your Skills

As you read, keep track of what happens first, next, and last. Sometimes clue words like *in the morning* can help you put events in order. Other times there are no clue words to help you. Put these events in order:
1. Beth was a painter.
2. Beth was a dancer.
3. Beth broke her ankle.

Look for time clues when you read about "The Big Orange Splot."

The Big Orange Splot

by Daniel Manus Pinkwater

Mr. Plumbean lived on a street where all the houses were the same. He liked it that way. So did everybody else on his street.

"This is a neat street," they would say.

Then one day a seagull flew over Mr. Plumbean's house. It was carrying a can of bright orange paint. (No one knows why.) And it dropped the can (no one knows why) right over Mr. Plumbean's house. The paint made a big orange splot on Mr. Plumbean's house.

"Ooooh! Too bad!" everybody said. "Mr. Plumbean will have to paint his house again."

"I suppose I will," said Mr. Plumbean. But he didn't paint his house right away. He looked at the big orange splot for a long time. Then he went about his everyday life.

The neighbors got tired of seeing that big orange splot. Someone said, "Mr. Plumbean, we wish you'd get around to painting your house."

"OK," said Mr. Plumbean.

He got some blue paint and some white paint. That night he got busy. He painted at night because it was cooler.

When the paint was gone, the roof was blue. The walls were white. And the big orange splot was still there.

Then he got some more paint. He got red paint, yellow paint, green paint, and purple paint.

In the morning, the other people on the street came out of their houses. Their houses were all the same. But Mr. Plumbean's house was like a rainbow. It was like a jungle. It was like an explosion.

There was the big orange splot. And there were little orange splots. There were stripes. There were pictures of elephants and lions and steamshovels.

The people said, "Plumbean has flipped his lid and blown his stack." They went away muttering.

That day Mr. Plumbean bought carpenter's tools. That night he built a tower on top of his roof. Then he painted a clock on the tower.

The next day the people said, "Plumbean has lost his marbles." They decided they would pretend not to notice.

That very night Mr. Plumbean got a truck full of green things. He planted palm trees and thorn bushes. In the morning he bought a table, some chairs, and an alligator.

When the other people came out of their houses, they saw Mr. Plumbean sitting under two palm trees. They saw an alligator in the grass. Mr. Plumbean was drinking lemonade.

"Plumbean has gone too far! This used to be a neat street! Plumbean, what have you done to your house?" the people shouted.

"My house is me, and I am it. My house is where I like to be, and it looks like all my dreams," Mr. Plumbean said.

The people went away. They asked the man who lived next door to Mr. Plumbean to talk with him. "Tell him that we all liked it here before he changed his house. Tell him that his house has to be the same as ours so we can have a neat street."

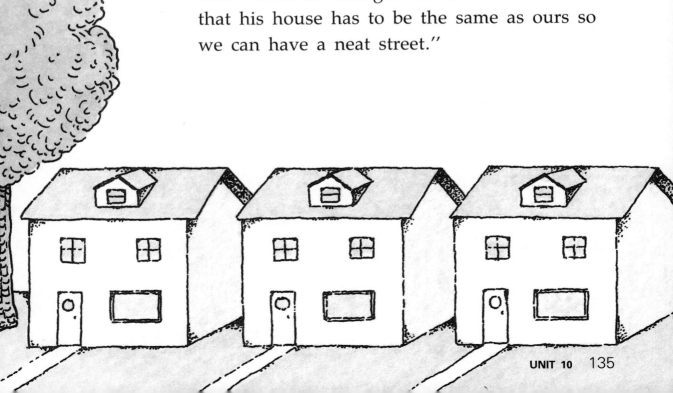

The man went to see Mr. Plumbean that evening. They sat under the palm trees, drinking lemonade and talking all night long.

Early the next morning the man went out to get lumber and rope and nails and paint. When the people came out of their houses, they saw a red-and-yellow ship next door to the house of Mr. Plumbean.

"What have you done to your house?" they shouted at the man.

"My house is me, and I am it. My house is where I like to be, and it looks like all my dreams," said the man, who had always loved ships.

"He's just like Plumbean!" the people said. "He's got bees in his bonnet and bats in his hat!"

Then, one by one, they went to see Mr. Plumbean, late at night. They would sit under the palm trees and drink lemonade and talk about their dreams. Whenever anybody visited Mr. Plumbean's house, the very next day that person would set about changing his own house to fit his dreams.

Whenever a stranger came to the street of Mr. Plumbean and his neighbors, the stranger would say, "This is not a neat street."

Then all the people would answer, "Our street is us, and we are it. Our street is where we like to be, and it looks like all our dreams."

Checking Comprehension and Skills

1. Why do you think Mr. Plumbean didn't paint his house right away?
2. Why do you think Mr. Plumbean's neighbors felt his house had to be like the others?
3. Was it right for Mr. Plumbean to change his house if the neighbors wanted the houses to be the same? Why do you think as you do?
•4. Put the following story events in order.
  a. The houses on the block were all alike.
  b. The houses were all different.
  c. Mr. Plumbean's house looked different from anyone else's.
•5. What house changed first? second? third?
  a. the next-door neighbor's house
  b. all the other neighbors' houses
  c. Mr. Plumbean's house

  Which word would you use in each sentence?
○6. She bought some ＿＿ to make a bookcase.
  chickens   lumber   purple
○7. He put the ＿＿ on the baby's head.
  suppose   rainbow   bonnet

• Sequence: Time sequence   ○ Structure: Syllables

Is It *Really* What It Looks Like?

These buildings used to have plain brick walls. Look at how artists have painted them!

Why would anyone paint a building to look like something different?

Music! Music!

Music! Music!

Music is everywhere: people playing music, people listening to music, and people writing music. There are so many kinds of music that everyone can find some music to enjoy. What kind of music do you enjoy?

From Start to Stars

As young girls in a small town in Illinois, Claire, Kristin, and Cathy Massey loved to sing. But they had no idea then that one day they would be rock stars.

Like other children at their school, the girls sang in school shows. When they were teenagers, they sang at family parties. They also started going to rock shows. The three girls dreamed that one day *they* might be on stage.

One summer the girls decided to put an act together. They had no trouble singing in front of strangers at a nearby pizza place. But they had learned enough songs for only one night.

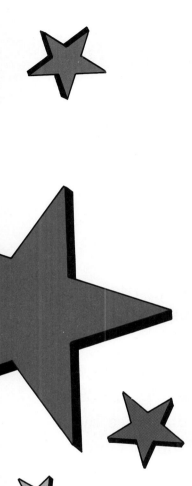

Soon after that, they went back to school. Claire and Kristin went on to college. Cathy went back to high school.

Three years later, the young women decided to get together again. They began singing with a band. Finally, with three friends, they started their own group—a rock band called "Sirenz." The group performs often at concerts and night spots in Chicago.

The three sisters plan to keep singing and to make records. As Cathy says, "We are living out our dream."

Sharpen Your Skills

Articles often are written in the time order that events happened, from first to last. Clue words like *as young girls* and *three years later* can help you keep track of the order of events.

1. About how old do you think Claire, Kristin, and Cathy were at the beginning of the article? What words help you figure this out?
2. About how old are the Masseys at the end?

When you read the next two articles, look for the order in which things happen.

Musically: Patrice Rushen

by Ohaji Abdallah

People love to hear Patrice Rushen play the piano during a concert or on a record. But they sometimes wonder how this young woman learned to play so well.

"Well, I started when I was three years old," Patrice remembers. "I was just big enough to reach the keys from the piano stool."

She also was too young to understand the notes that musicians use to read music. "So our teacher taught us to learn the notes by the way they sounded. Dotted notes were called skipping notes because they made you think of skipping. I still think of music like that today when I play."

Patrice says that she plays all kinds of music. But most of all, she just plays "music with feeling." "I always play music that will make other people feel something. That's something that I picked up from those classes when I was three."

For a long time, Patrice didn't try to sing. Now she sings on many of her records. "I had to practice the piano. I had to do the same with singing," she says. "I have taken lessons and that helped. I think it is important for anyone who wants to be a singer or a musician to understand one thing. If you want to do something well, you have to work hard at it."

After years of struggle, Patrice is now a well-known singer and musician. She also writes songs. Patrice has recorded more than twenty albums.

From Ox Horn to Bugle and Then Some

by Roger McCain

There is an old saying that you cannot make a silk purse out of a pig's ear. If that's true, an ox horn could not become a bugle. But, in fact, that is just what did happen.

The word *bugle* is French for "ox horn." It was called that because the first horns that people played were made from animal horns. The horns came from animals, such as oxen and cows.

For thousands of years, people played animal horns. Their loud sound could be heard from far away. The horns were used to call the people of a village together. They were also used by armies in battle.

Later, horns were made of metal, such as brass. But they were still called bugles. They were still used by armies, both in training and in battle. They were also used by hunters in the field and by members of bands.

Most brass bugles could play just five notes. In the early 1800s, Joseph Halliday, who was the leader of a band, changed the bugle. He added five keys to it. A bugle with keys could play twenty-five notes, and it still had its loud sound.

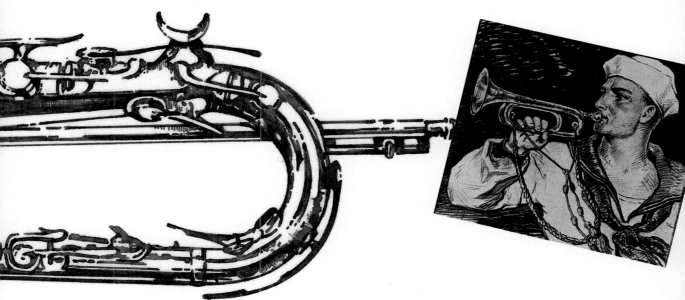

The key bugle quickly became very well-known. In America, it became important in bands. It was played in army and navy bands, police and fire bands, and school and town bands.

Today bugles may not be quite as important as they once were. But they still play a part in the world of music. They are often used to awaken people in scout and army camps. They are also used in both places to play "Taps" at the end of each day. Hearing "Taps" played on a bugle means it's time to put out the lights.

Checking Comprehension and Skills

1. What kind of music does Patrice Rushen say she likes to play? (144)
2. How can you tell that Patrice worked hard to become a good musician?
3. Do you think it is good for children to start music lessons as young as Patrice did? Why do you think as you do?
4. If Patrice wanted to become a bugle player, what advice would she give herself?
●5. Put the following events in order.
   a. Patrice took her first piano lesson.
   b. Patrice played the piano and sang on her records.
   c. Patrice learned to play the piano well.
●6. Put the following events in order.
   a. Keys were added to brass bugles.
   b. People played animal horns.
   c. Horns were made of metal.
7. What did you learn about bugles that you didn't know before?

   Which word would you use in this sentence?
○8. The ____ began when the bugle sounded.
   battle   apple   little

● Sequence: Time sequence   ○ Structure: Syllables

Sculpture

Do you know what this picture is? It looks like something you might eat. But it is too big to eat. It would not taste good either. It is really a piece of sculpture. A person made it out of cloth.

Sculpture can be made of different things. It can be made of stone, wood, cloth, or even paper. Sculpture can show people, things that happened, or ideas. It can be very serious. Or, it can make you laugh.

When you make something out of mud, rocks, or wood, *you* are making sculpture too.

Giant Hamburger, by Claes Oldenburg,
ART GALLERY OF ONTARIO, TORONTO, Purchase, 1967

Following the Steps in a Process

Pablo made his own spider-web sculpture. By looking at the pictures, you can see the steps he followed. What were they?

Sharpen Your Skills

Sometimes you have to read to find out how to make something. To make it right, you must follow the directions. Here's how:

• Look ahead. See if there is a picture of what you'll end up with. This will help you see where the steps are taking you.

• Then read and follow the directions. If the steps aren't numbered, look for clue words like *first, next, while,* and *last* that tell you when to do each step.

1

2 3

Pablo also made a dragon. To find out how he made this sculpture, read the next paragraph. Look for clue words that tell what he did first.

To begin, Pablo drew a picture of a dragon. Then he got some cardboard boxes and colored paper. Pablo chose the biggest box to be the dragon's body. After that, he glued on smaller boxes to make the head, feet, and tail. He cut eyes, ears, and wings out of paper. Finally, he glued them in place.

1. What did Pablo do first?
2. What clue words helped you answer?

Pablo drew a picture of a dragon first, before he even started the sculpture. Did the clue words *To begin* help you? Reread the paragraph about Pablo's dragon to answer the following questions.

3. Which did Pablo do last—glue the smaller boxes to the body or glue on the eyes, ears, and wings?
4. What clue word helped you answer?

As you read about Deborah Butterfield, watch for the steps she followed in making a horse.

Deborah Butterfield: Sculptor

by Hannah Loop

Deborah Butterfield is a sculptor who makes statues of horses. Her horses look and feel different from most horse statues you might have seen.

Butterfield makes her horses out of things found at horse farms. She uses old wire and boards from fences. She uses large pieces of iron from barns. She puts these things together in the shape of a horse.

Butterfield made the horse in the picture on page 156. His name is Ponder.

Before she built Ponder, Butterfield spent months thinking about a group of horses she wanted to make. While she was building Ponder, her own horse died. Suddenly, making Ponder was a very important project. The love she had felt for her own horse went into finishing Ponder.

Butterfield built a frame for the horse's body. She made it out of steel. When she thought it looked right, she hung it from the ceiling. Then she built the horse's legs.

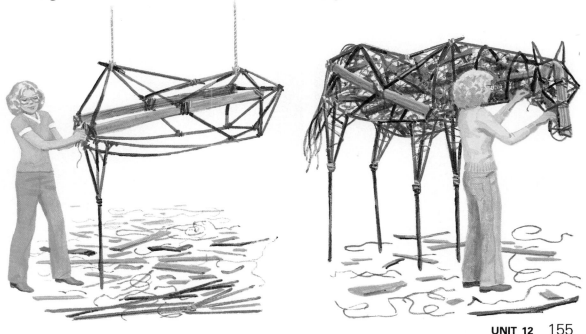

After the legs were put on, the frame could stand on the ground by itself. But it still needed a neck and head. The neck and head were put on. Now Ponder's frame was finished.

Butterfield began to stuff the statue. She shoved pieces of wire and small sticks inside the frame.

How did Butterfield know when Ponder was finished? "When I couldn't make him any better," she said. She was right. Ponder looks perfect just the way he is.

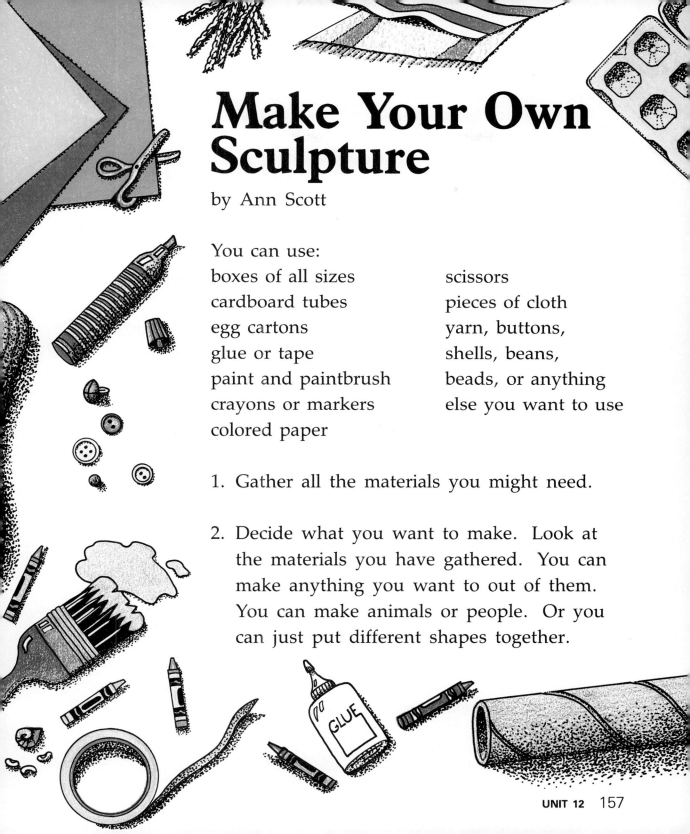

Make Your Own Sculpture

by Ann Scott

You can use:

boxes of all sizes
cardboard tubes
egg cartons
glue or tape
paint and paintbrush
crayons or markers
colored paper

scissors
pieces of cloth
yarn, buttons,
shells, beans,
beads, or anything
else you want to use

1. Gather all the materials you might need.

2. Decide what you want to make. Look at the materials you have gathered. You can make anything you want to out of them. You can make animals or people. Or you can just put different shapes together.

3. Draw a rough picture of what you have in mind.

4. Cut your materials to the sizes and shapes you want.

5. Glue or tape the materials together.

6. Paint your sculpture—all of it or parts.

7. Glue buttons, shells, beans, beads, pieces of cloth, or anything else on your sculpture.

Look at what some children have made.

Susan has made a pony out of tubes.

Marcus has made a model of a rabbit.

Checking Comprehension and Skills

1. Why was making Ponder an important project for Deborah Butterfield? (155)

•2. Put in order these three steps that Butterfield went through to build Ponder.

  a. She put the legs on the frame.

  b. She built the frame.

  c. She put the neck and head on the frame.

•3. Why is Step 2 on page 157 one of the most important steps in making a sculpture?

4. Do you like the sculpture of Ponder and the sculptures on this page? Why or why not?

Which word would you use in this sentence?

○5. A _____ looks like a small horse.

  glider   pony   cabin

• Sequence: Steps in a process
○ Structure: Syllables

Reading Math Word Problems

If you played an army bugle, you would not play the same way for a battle as for "lights out." You also would not read a math word problem the same way you would read a story. To read word problems, use these tips:

- Read the problem carefully. Ask, "What is the question? What facts are given?"
- Solve the problem. Ask, "What should I do first? next? last?"
- Answer the question. Then read it again. Ask, "Does my answer make sense?"

See how the tips help solve this problem:

- Read   Marla used 7 tubes to make a giraffe. How many tubes does Marla need to make 4 giraffes?

- Solve

Tubes needed		Number of giraffes		Total tubes
7	×	4	=	28

- Answer   She needs 28 tubes for 4 giraffes.

Use these tips when you read word problems.

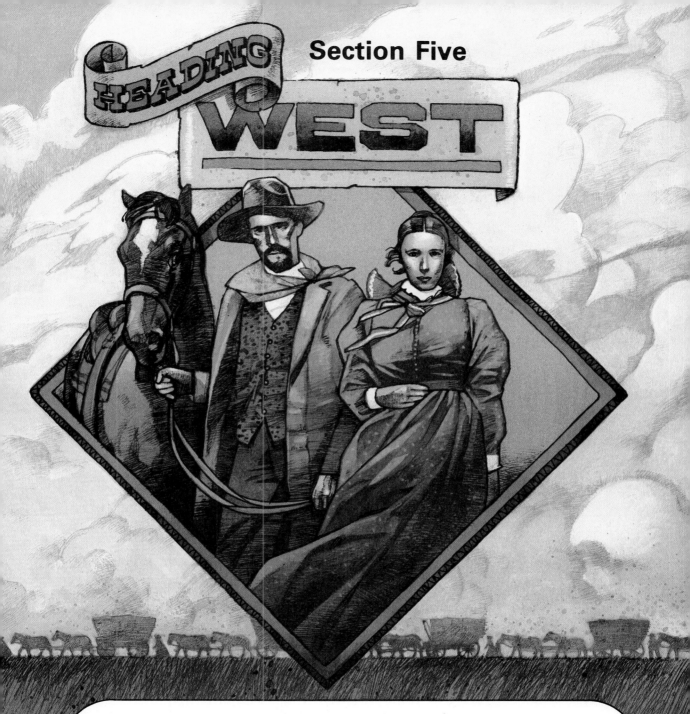

Section Five

HEADING WEST

Wagon Trains

Over one hundred years ago, many people left their homes and traveled west across the United States. Some families went looking for more land to farm. Others went all the way to California to look for gold. They all went in search of a better life.

Many people headed west in covered wagons. They traveled together in groups of wagons called wagon trains.

The trip was not easy. The people and animals on the wagon train faced danger. Many of them died before they reached their new homes. But people were so eager to start a new life that they went anyway.

On the Trail

Pilot and Blue were oxen. They were two of the four oxen pulling the Miller family's wagon. The Millers were part of a wagon train heading west from a town in Missouri.

"I think we are going to move soon," Pilot said to Blue.

"I can wait," said Blue. "Today is going to be terrible."

"As miserable as ever," Pilot added.

"Come on, old boys," Mrs. Miller called out to the oxen. "Let's roll."

Pilot and Blue took a few steps. The wagon jumped forward. Soon the wagon was moving down the trail.

"The bugs are bad today," Pilot said.

"And the air is dark with trail dust already," said Blue.

"That's because we're at the back of the train. I liked being in the front yesterday. The air was clear," said Pilot.

"Well, today can't be as bad as that rainy day last week. The wagon got stuck in the mud," Blue said. "And *we* had to pull it out."

"How far do you think we'll go today?" Pilot asked.

"About fourteen miles," Blue answered. "When we reach the river, we'll stop. Then we can eat and drink."

"And rest," Pilot added. "I sure hope we reach the river without any trouble."

Sharpen Your Skills

When you read a story that is made up by a writer, you are reading **fiction.** The characters may seem to be real, but the author has made up how they look, what they say, and what they do.

1. What details in "On the Trail" seem real?
2. What lets you know that the author made up the story?

Look for details that show that "Trouble for Lucy" is fiction. It was made up by Carla Stevens.

From TROUBLE FOR LUCY

by Carla Stevens

Lucy Stewart is traveling to Oregon in a wagon train with her family. One morning something terrible happens. Her dog, Finn, disappears.

"Finn! Here, Finn!" Lucy's high voice caused heads to turn in her direction. Suddenly she spotted her friend Miles.

"Miles!" she said. "I can't find my dog anywhere."

"I'll help you look," Miles said.

Lucy and Miles stopped at each wagon to ask if anyone had seen a little black-and-white

puppy. When they reached the end of the
wagon train, they had seen many dogs, but
not Finn.

"Oh, Miles, do you suppose he was left
behind where we set up camp last night?"

"No, I'm sure not," Miles said firmly.
"Someone would have seen him."

"But what if they didn't see him? What
then?" She said suddenly, "I'm going back to
the campground and check to be sure."

"But, Lucy, you can't do that! It's going to
rain." Miles looked up at the heavy gray
clouds moving swiftly across the sky.

"I'll be back." Lucy patted Miles's arm.
"Don't worry."

She turned and began running. In just a
few minutes she had left Miles far behind.

The wind blew harder. Lucy stopped for a
moment and looked back at the wagon train.
She could still see the wagons, but now they
looked like specks. The sky to the west was
heavy with black clouds. Was that a drop of
rain? She began to run again. Ahead, she
could see where they had made camp last night.

"Finn!" she called. "Here, Finn!"

She felt a sharp and biting sting. Hailstones! A clap of thunder rolled overhead. Now the hailstones began falling faster, bouncing off her head and shoulders.

Lucy ran and crawled under the first willow bush she saw. Leaning down, she covered her head with her arms to protect herself from the pelting hailstones.

"I can't stay here," she whispered. "I must start back." She lifted her head. She screamed Finn's name. Until this moment she had always believed she would find her puppy. But now she was not so certain.

Was that a bark? Or just the noisy rumble of the hailstones? She crawled out from under the bush and began to move toward the sound. "Finn! Here, Finn!"

A real bark answered her call. Ahead, she saw something move under a bush. It *was* Finn.

When Finn saw Lucy, he began barking and wagging his tail. "Oh, Finn. What happened to you?" The thorns on the bush cut and tore at Lucy's hands when she picked him up.

The hailstones had begun to turn into rain. "I must get started back this minute," she thought. "It won't be easy to catch up when the ground is so muddy."

She began to follow the ruts made by the wagon wheels through the wet prairie grass. Finn ran along happily beside her. The rain was turning into a drizzle. Ahead, toward the west, she saw a patch of blue sky appear through the clouds. But the wagon train was not in sight.

Lucy stopped and listened. She could hear a muffled sound that grew louder by the minute. It was coming from across the river. Looking in that direction, she saw a small group of people on horseback riding toward her. Her heart jumped. Were they Indians?

Lucy began to run faster along the trail, tripping and stumbling as she watched the horses come closer. Now they were crossing the river. Yes, they were Indians. She could see the brown-and-white markings on their ponies.

"Finn! Come here!" she said sharply. The puppy ran to her. She picked him up and held him tightly as the ponies galloped toward her. There were five men.

The men were laughing and talking among themselves in a strange language. They halted their ponies around Lucy. One young man spoke to her. Shaking her head, Lucy said, "I can't understand you."

She held up Finn and pointed back toward last night's camp. She pointed to the tracks made by the wagon wheels, then to the west. "My wagon train is there," she said.

For the first time, the young man who had spoken to her smiled at her. Saying a few words, he leaned toward her and held out his hand. Then he gently patted the place in front of him on his horse and pointed at Finn.

For a moment Lucy hesitated. Then she stood on her toes and held Finn up to him. "Here," she said. The young man took Finn, smiled, and leaned down. He reached out his other hand and spoke softly to her again.

Lucy held her arms up to him and felt herself being pulled onto the horse. As soon as she was on, the man handed her the puppy.

The man waved and signaled to the others to follow. Then he turned his horse and began galloping toward the west.

They galloped on and on, faster than she had ever galloped before. Then Lucy saw a line of black ants on the horizon. She laughed, knowing that they weren't really ants at all.

"Look!" she pointed ahead. "There's the wagon train!"

Soon they were riding past wagon after wagon. She tugged at the man's coat. The Indian slowed down his horse just as Lucy saw Miles walking beside his oxen.

"Miles!" she called out. "I found Finn!"

Miles stared at the Indians, and his eyes grew big and round.

Lucy pulled at the Indian's coat again. "I want to get down," she said.

The young man pulled his horse to a halt. Lucy gave Finn to the man. She half slid, half jumped off the horse's back. She reached up and took Finn from the man just before he rode off.

Miles was so excited he hopped up and down. "Weren't you scared, Lucy?" he asked. "I mean about those Indians."

"I was scared when I first saw them because they were strangers," Lucy said honestly. "But I would never have caught up with the wagon train if they hadn't found me."

"You have all the luck. I sure would like to have ridden on an Indian pony," said Miles.

Checking Comprehension and Skills

1. What did Lucy want at the beginning of the story? How did she get it? (166-167)
2. How did Lucy feel when she first saw the Indians? Why? How did she feel when they brought her back? (172)
3. Was it brave or was it foolish of Lucy to go back for Finn? Why do you think that?
•4. "Trouble for Lucy" is fiction. What details would help you know that?
•5. On page 168, the author writes about a hailstorm. What details make it seem real?
6. Imagine you are a pioneer. What would you like and dislike about going west? Why?

Which word under each sentence means the same as the underlined word in the sentence?

∘7. The puppy kept tripping over its own feet.
   stumbling   eating   walking
∘8. Everyone waved for the wagon to stop.
   galloped   signaled   laughed

• Fiction   ∘ Synonyms and antonyms

Great
Plains

New Land, New Life

Many families headed west to look for good land to farm. They found it when they got to the Great Plains of the United States.

Pretend you and your family are traveling through the Great Plains one hundred years ago. When you arrive at the land your family wants, nothing is there. You see no roads, no buildings, no farms nearby. Everywhere you look, you see empty land filled only with tall, waving grass.

How do you begin your new life? What do you do first?

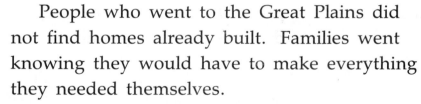

People who went to the Great Plains did not find homes already built. Families went knowing they would have to make everything they needed themselves.

When a family arrived at their land, the first job was to build a place to live. The family slept in a wagon or tent until something more lasting could be built. A home had to be made right away. If it weren't built before winter, the family could die in the cold weather.

The two most common kinds of homes were dugouts and sod houses.

A dugout was a hole dug out of the ground. It was usually dug in the side of a small hill. When the hole was big enough, a front wall was made out of sod.

Sod was the building material of the plains. It was a piece of ground covered with thick grass. It didn't cost anything, and there was plenty of it.

A sod house was made by cutting the ground into thick strips. Then the strips were put on top of one another like bricks. The sod house, or "soddy," was warm enough for a family to live in through the worst winter.

Sharpen Your Skills

Sometimes you read articles that give you facts about real people, places, things, and events. These articles are **nonfiction. Fiction,** on the other hand, is about people and events made up by a writer.

1. "A New Home, Fast" is nonfiction. How can you tell?
2. What are two facts about sod houses that you learned when you read this article?

As you read the next two stories, decide whether each is fiction or nonfiction.

Life in a Soddy

by Paul Quinn

Great Plains, a large, flat part of the United States east of the Rocky Mountains

Most of the **Great Plains** settlers had lived in wood houses before they moved west. Living in a sod house was different from living in a wood house, and it took getting used to.

The Chrisman sisters and their sod house in Nebraska

The settlers built their sod homes to be warm and tight. The sod walls were three feet[1] thick. They kept out the snow and cold of winter. They also kept out the heat of the summer. But they didn't keep out the bugs and small animals that lived on the plains.

Sod roofs were often a problem. Spring rains caused the roofs to leak. When they leaked, they didn't drip clean water. They leaked mud.

Even in good weather, bits and pieces of a sod roof could fall down. The cook always had to cover the pots on the stove!

The floor of a sod house was bare earth. It was easy to keep clean once the settler learned to sprinkle water on it before sweeping. That made the floor as hard as rock. But dirt floors had problems too. A heavy rain would turn them into mud puddles.

Sod houses were plain. Usually they had only one room. That room was used as the kitchen, bedroom, dining room, and living room. The contents were just as simple. A bed and a table, some chairs, and a few dishes were all that were needed.

By the Way
Since there were living plants in the sod roofs, the roofs often were covered with wild flowers in the spring.

Facts and Figures
Sod was free, and wood was cheap in those days. One settler figured his whole sod house had cost him $2.78½ to build.

---

1. about one meter

Once the sod house, or "soddy," was built, a pioneer family had more hard work to do. They had to grow and cook all the food for the family to eat. Water and fuel for the stove had to be found and carried to the house. The farm animals and crops had to be cared for.

Many dangers had to be faced when living on the plains. There were dust storms, wind storms, and fire storms. There were blizzards, and there were long months that went by without rain.

A fire storm on the prairie

The life of pioneers was not all danger and hardship. They found plenty of time for fun. Many of their parties were built around work. Sometimes people got together to build a soddy for a new family. Other parties were just for fun. Dances and singing parties were common.

There were good reasons why many pioneers were content with their lives on the plains. They had the chance of owning their own farms. The land was beautiful. The plains offered adventure. And pioneers liked the feeling of being free.

Very few pioneers had cameras. Those who did earned money by taking pictures. The pictures became family treasures. Here is one family gathered in front of their soddy.

COMPANY

by
Jane
Whitehead

Karl Gunther and his pa were climbing
down from the sod roof when Ma called them
and Karl's two sisters to supper. At last
they had finished building their soddy!

Two months ago, the Gunther family had
left Ohio in a covered wagon to live in the
west. Neither Karl nor his sisters liked
the plains. Their nearest neighbors were more
than an hour's ride away. There was just grass
waving in the wind. There was always a wind.

That night after supper, Karl and Pa went
out to feed the cow and horses. The wind
was blowing stronger. Lightning flashed.

Pa looked at the sky. "We finished the
roof just in time, didn't we?"

Inside, Ma had cleared the table and
spread Karl's blankets on it. He climbed
under them and fell asleep at once.

Suddenly Karl woke up. His face was wet.
He heard raindrops hissing as they hit the
stove. It was a rainstorm—inside! They all
grabbed blankets and ran out to the wagon.
It was warm and dry inside the wagon.

The next morning Karl climbed out of the wagon. He walked over to the house and opened the door. Then he shut it fast. "Pa!" he cried. "It's still raining inside!"

Pa brought two shovels from the wagon. He handed one to Karl. "Dig a ditch from the doorway out to the tall grass." Pa dug a ditch in the floor from the doorway to the opposite wall of the house. Then he dug another one across the room.

Slowly the water ran into the ditches. It flowed out the doorway and into the tall grass. It took three days to dry out the house and fix the roof.

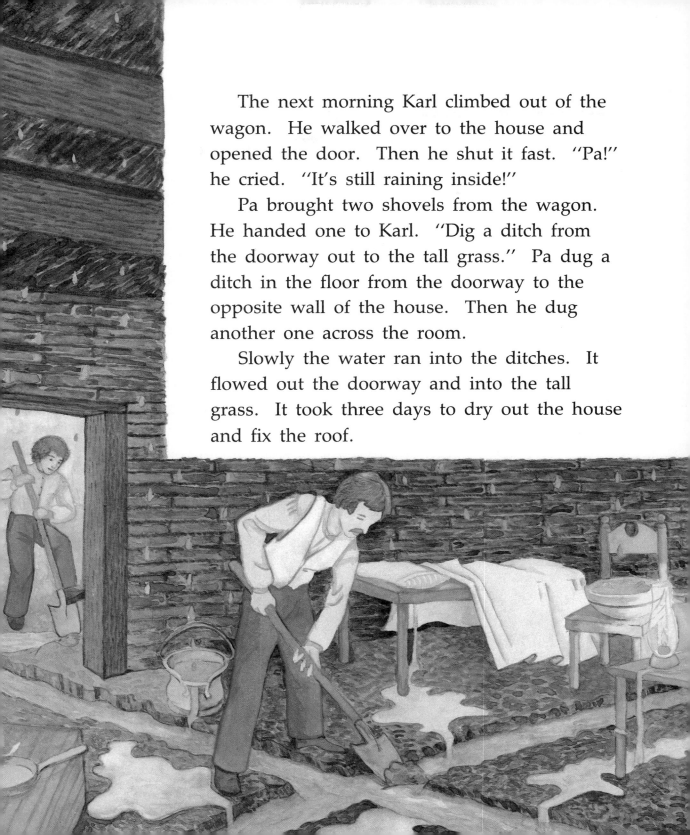

Karl hoped it would *never* rain again. Every day he went outside to look at the sky. Then one morning he saw a wagon coming toward the soddy.

When the wagon stopped at the door, a tall man jumped out and said, "Welcome, neighbors! I'm Bill Dumond. This is my wife, Claire, and my son, Pete." He shook Pa's hand.

Pete walked over to Karl. "Our dog had puppies. You can have one if you want one. What's your name? Will you be my friend?"

Karl grinned, nodded, and started talking to Pete. Everyone had a wonderful day.

The Gunthers waved from the doorway when the Dumonds started home. Karl started to close the door, but he stopped and shouted, "Hey, Pete! We'll never be *close* friends!"

Pete looked surprised, then laughed. "You're right. We'll have to be far-apart friends!"

Checking Comprehension and Skills

•1. Was "Life in a Soddy" nonfiction or fiction? Why do you think as you do?

2. What are two ways in which living in a sod house was different from living in a wood house? (179)

3. Which sentence gives the main idea of the last paragraph on page 180?   the first paragraph on 181?

4. Do you think life in a soddy was easier or harder than life today? How?

5. How was the sod hut the Gunthers built like the homes in "Life in a Soddy"?

•6. Was "Company" fiction or nonfiction? Why do you think as you do?

7. Would you like living in a soddy? Why?

What does <u>close</u> mean in each sentence?

○8. It was cold so I had to <u>close</u> the door.
shut   near

○9. The door is <u>close</u> to the window.
shut   near

• Fiction and nonfiction   ○ Homographs

The Gold Rush

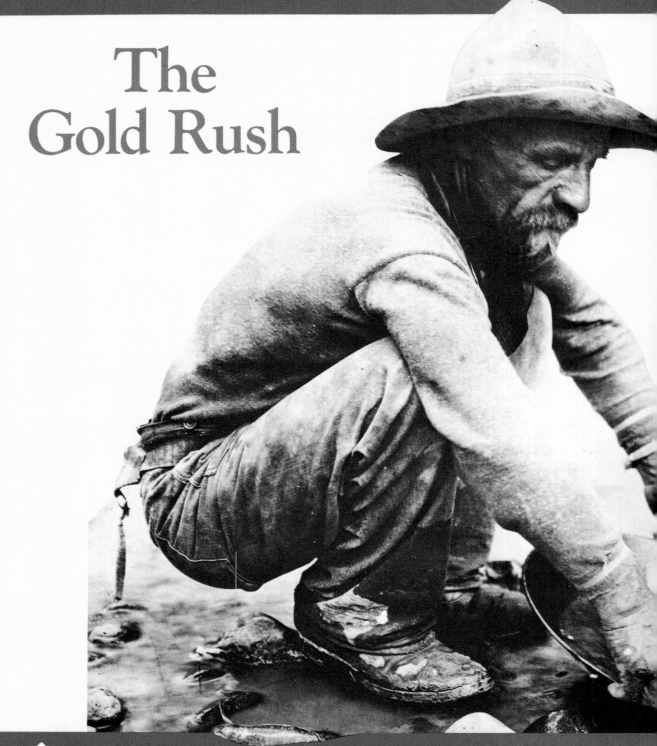

In 1847 California was a quiet place with few people living in it. But in January, 1848, a man found something shiny in the ground. It was gold!

For the next ten years, thousands and thousands of people rushed to California to look for gold.

Life in the mountain gold camps was hard. Most people found only enough gold to pay for their food and tools. But people kept coming. They all hoped they would be lucky enough to "strike it rich."

Using a Map

Carla's family drove from their home in Palo Alto, California, to Sacramento. At the hotel, Carla found a map of Sacramento. Most of all, she wanted to see Sutter's Fort. That's where many people went to look for gold in 1849.

How will Carla and her family get to the fort? Look at the map below.

SACRAMENTO

Sharpen Your Skills

A **map** helps people get from one place to another. It is often easier to tell where things are by looking at a map than by reading words. The **key** shows what the pictures on the map stand for. Find the picture that stands for the fort. Do you see that picture on the map itself?

Now find the **direction arrows.** They show which way is north, south, east, or west.

1. The hotel is at the corner of which streets?
2. Should Carla's family drive east or west to get from the hotel to the fort?

The hotel is at Seventh and K Streets. Did you find the picture there? Carla's family will drive east to get to the fort. Now use the key and the arrows to answer these questions.

3. After seeing the fort, Carla's family wants to see the State Capitol buildings. Which way will they drive—east or west?
4. What streets would they use to get from the Capitol buildings to the hotel?

Use the maps as you read "Backward."

Backward

by Sharon Fear

Uncle Seth got off his mule. He helped
Mary get off hers. Traveling from Illinois to
California by wagon and mule had taken
months. Mary and her uncle were tired.

Mary looked unhappily at the dusty main
street. It was noisy with horses and wagons.
Many people in dusty clothes led mules
loaded down with miners' tools.

Mary and her uncle took their bags off the
mules. They went straight to Mr. Wood's
office. Mr. Wood was the lawyer who had
written Mary about her father's death.

Mr. Wood didn't waste any time explaining the will Mary's father had left. "Since you are a minor, Mary, your uncle will take care of you. Your father left these things for you," said the lawyer. "The first is this map."

Mary and her uncle studied it. It was a simple map, showing directions from town to a place marked X.

"Frankly," said Mr. Wood, "I don't understand it. Some of these places just are not there. There's no such lake north of town." He pointed to one on the map.

"The other thing your father left you, Mary, is a letter," said Mr. Wood. "Your father told me you have trouble reading. Shall I read it to you?"

"Please," said Mary. At ten years of age, after lots of hard work, Mary could read. But it was still hard. She thought she saw writing differently from other people. It seemed to her that some words were backwards. Some letters even seemed upside down.

"My darling Mary," the lawyer read. "Besides my love, I have only one thing to leave you. This map will take you to it. Remember the song I wrote for you. Your loving father."

Mr. Wood handed the letter and map to Mary. "I hope you can make some sense out of this. I certainly can't."

Mary thanked the lawyer and left the office with her uncle. They walked down the street to the boarding house. Uncle Seth shook his head.

"He didn't even have five cents to leave you," he said. "All he gave you was a map that nobody understands—a map to nowhere."

After dropping off their bags at the boarding house, Mary and Uncle Seth went on to the cemetery. It was easy to find the grave. Someone had put a board on the grave and painted her father's name on it.

Uncle Seth cried. Mary wanted to, but couldn't.

Walking back from the cemetery, Mary said, "I know how to read Father's map. His letter said to remember the song. He wrote it for me when I was having trouble reading." Then Mary sang this song for Uncle Seth.

North is south, and east is west.
My girl thinks that backward's best.
Left is right, and high is low.
Some say Mary's mighty slow.
First is last, and up is down.
But she gets there by going 'round.

"That's it! It's a backward map!" said Uncle Seth.

"To go to the X," Mary said, "we'll do the opposite of what the directions tell us to do."

The next day they hired fresh mules and bought food. Then they rode out of town. The map said ride north, so they rode south. The map said take the west fork. They took the east fork.

The second day out, they came to the spot marked "Lake" on the map.

"There's the lake," said her uncle, looking at it. "The map says go east to two pine trees. Then it says go to the west of the rock with eyes. So we'll go in the opposite directions."

They went west. In the shade of two tall pines, they tied the mules. They climbed up toward a huge rock with holes like eyes. On the east side of it, well hidden, was a cave.

In the dim light inside the cave, they saw a bedroll beside a cold campfire. A coffee pot, a tin cup, a miner's pick, and some candles were there too. Mary looked at her father's things. The tears that would not come at his grave came now.

"Come and look, Mary." Uncle Seth was in the back of the cave. He was holding a candle up to the rocky wall. She went in and looked. Spots of white and yellow glittered in the candlelight.

"I'm a farmer, not a miner," said Uncle Seth. "But I think that's gold."

That night they talked by the campfire.

"I thought your dad was crazy to come west. I was wrong. He was smart, the way he drew that map." Uncle Seth looked across the fire at Mary. "And he knew you would figure it out."

She smiled. "A backward map for a backward girl."

"There's nothing backward about you," he said. "No one knew that better than your dad."

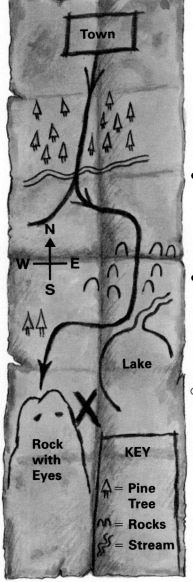

Town

N
W——E
S

Lake

Rock
with
Eyes

KEY

🌲 = Pine
Tree

〰 = Rocks

𝔰 = Stream

1. What is the setting of "Backward"? (190)
2. Mary's father left a message. What was the message?
3. How did Mary's father keep it secret?
4. Do you think Mary's father was crazy or smart for going west? Why do you think so?
5. What kind of girl do you think Mary is?
•6. On the backward map on page 191, the rocks are north and west of town. Where are the rocks on the real map shown on this page?
•7. On the map on page 191, the lake is north of the rocks. Where was the lake? (196)
8. Now that Mary and Uncle Seth have found the gold mine, what do you think they will do?
○9. Read the next sentence, then fill in the blanks.
The <u>two</u> miners found gold, and silver <u>too</u>.
<u>Two</u> means ____.
along with   the number 2   very
<u>Too</u> means ____.
the number 2   also   as far as

• Graphic Aids: Maps   ○ Homophones

Panning for Gold

Panning is one way of finding gold. The idea of panning is to make the gold, which is very heavy, sink to the bottom of a pan of dirt. Then you wash away the dirt.

You can try panning for gold in a mountain stream. This is how to do it.

1. Put some sand and dirt from the bottom of the stream into a pie pan. Take out any stones with no dirt on them.

2. Cover the sand and dirt with water. Tilt the pan a bit. Shake the pan so that the dirt moves back and forth in the water. Do this for about a minute. This makes the gold settle to the bottom of the dirt. Then let the dirt settle in one end of the pan.

3. Put the pan in calm water. Carefully move the pan around in the water so the water carries away some dirt. Do this three times.

4. Do steps 2 and 3 again. Repeat these steps until there is mostly black sand in the pan. Then look through the sand for little flakes of gold. Take them out with the wet tip of a brush and put them into a small jar with water in it.

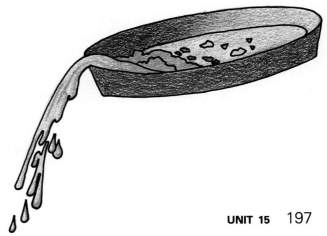

Questions You Can Ask Yourself

If you just saw the first picture, you might wonder, "Why is everyone carrying an umbrella into the house?" The answer is in the second picture.

You will get more from your reading if you ask questions as you read. This helps you understand each part of a story. As you read "Backward," you might have asked yourself:

• Why did Mary's father give her such a strange map?

• What did the X stand for?

You would have found answers in the story.

Asking questions and finding answers helps you figure out what's important. Try it the next time you read.

Water Worlds

Beauty Under the Water

People like to sit on the beach and look at the beauty of the ocean. They enjoy watching the waves, the sea birds, and the fish that sometimes come to the surface.

The ocean is also very beautiful under its surface. Brightly colored plants grow on its floor. Water animals with beautiful shells crawl over sand and rocks. Fish in every size, shape, and color slip through the water. Some of them don't even look like fish!

To enjoy all of the ocean's beauty, people have found ways to explore under its surface.

Underwater Dance

The summer day was warm and beautiful. The ocean sparkled blue and green in the sun. The air smelled fresh.

"I ought to be happy and excited," said Dina as she sat on the edge of the boat. "But I'm really scared to death."

"We've been taking diving lessons for weeks," said her friend Cindy. "This is no different from all our other dives."

"The other dives were practice," replied Dina. "We did those in a swimming pool. This is the ocean!"

"Well, I want to go in," said Cindy. "Come on. I need a partner. Get ready."

"Ready?" thought Dina. "I'll never be ready! How did I ever get into this?"

Just then a large school of shiny, silver fish glided by. They gracefully zigzagged through the water. The green leaves of an underwater plant floated and drifted among the fish.

"How beautiful," sighed Dina. "It's like a gentle underwater dance." And at that moment Dina knew why she had come. With her air tank and mask on, she jumped into the water. Dina knew she wanted to be part of that beautiful underwater world.

Sharpen Your Skills

To tell what a story is all about, figure out who the story is about and what happens.

1. How does Dina feel when the story begins?
2. Which sentence tells what the story is all about?
   a. Dina got over her fear of diving.
   b. It was a warm, beautiful summer day.

When you finish "Walk Like a Duck, Swim Like a Fish," try to say what it is all about.

Walk Like a Duck, Swim Like a Fish

by Leonard Shortall

Nine-year-old Antonio lives near the ocean. He wants to learn to swim, but he is afraid. His parents think he ought to learn. So his mother sends him to swimming lessons.

Antonio and his older sister Luisa left for the beach. They were early, so they walked out to the end of the dock. Some of Luisa's friends were playing there.

Antonio noticed a boy in red trunks, who was noisier than the others. "I'm king of the castle," Red Trunks cried, as the children came near. Laughing, he pushed Antonio off the dock. Antonio fell into the water with a big splash!

From *Tony's First Dive* by Leonard Shortall. Copyright © 1972 by Leonard Shortall. Adapted by permission of William Morrow & Company.

Antonio was frightened as the cold water closed over his head. He kicked this way and that way. Down he went. He fought to hold his breath. At last he came back up again. Someone grabbed him.

"You're all right, Antonio! I've got you!" Luisa shouted.

Finally, Antonio could breathe again.

Luisa pulled Antonio to a ladder, and Antonio climbed up it. The other children gathered around him.

"How did I know he couldn't swim?" Red Trunks cried.

Antonio said that he was all right. Then he walked back to the beach and sat down on the sand. When he saw someone else push Red Trunks off the dock, he felt better.

Before long the beginners' swimming class began. Antonio went into the water with the other children. First the teacher asked them to put their faces underwater with their eyes open. Antonio tried. But the salt water stung his eyes so he kept them closed.

Then Antonio got water up his nose. He choked and lifted his head. Soon he started to shiver. At last he told the teacher that he didn't feel well. Slowly he waded ashore and walked home.

Every day that week, Antonio missed the swimming class for one reason or another.

At the end of the week Luisa and her friends planned a picnic out on Twin Island. Antonio wanted to go with them. But his mother said that he couldn't take a boat trip until he learned how to swim.

Antonio sat on the beach and watched the boats leave for the picnic. He felt sad.

Suddenly Antonio saw a figure in the water. A swimmer with a face mask was coming up for air. It was Dave Johnson, a lifeguard at the beach.

"Hello, Antonio," Dave said. He waded out of the water onto the beach.

While Dave rested for a moment, he let Antonio hold the face mask. It was made of thick rubber and glass. "Can you really see underwater with this?" Antonio asked.

"Come into the water and see for yourself," Dave answered. "When I wear it while I'm swimming, I see a lot of the interesting things that surround me."

Antonio followed Dave into the water until it reached his waist. Then he looked through the mask. He could see the bottom clearly, and his eyes didn't sting.

Antonio decided as he handed it back that he wanted a face mask too. "I wish I could swim," he said. He told Dave about the trouble he was having.

"Why don't I teach you?" Dave said. "We can start right now."

First, Dave told Antonio to hold his breath, bend over, and hold his ankles. When Antonio did this, he was floating. Next, Antonio learned how a swimmer breathes. Finally, Antonio put his face in the water, kicked with his feet, and paddled with his arms. He was swimming!

Antonio practiced swimming all week with Dave. Soon he stopped being afraid of the water. Antonio and his parents were pleased.

One morning his parents gave him a surprise—a face mask and a pair of swim fins. When Antonio went to the beach, he had on his fins, ready to swim.

"Antonio, you walk like a duck!" Red Trunks called.

When Dave was ready for him, Antonio walked like a duck into the water.

Out in the water, Antonio pulled his mask over his face. He held his breath. He put his head underwater and looked around. The mask worked fine! As he swam, he looked at the crabs and shells below. He was excited that he could see everything so clearly.

The next day Dave taught Antonio how to surface dive. Antonio learned to put his head underwater, bend in the middle, and swim straight to the bottom.

"Now you can dive like a duck as well as walk like one!" Dave told Antonio.

Then Antonio swam underwater a little way with Dave. Soon he went deeper and began to hold his breath longer. During the next few days, Antonio swam underwater a lot.

One morning Antonio walked out onto the dock. At the end of the dock, a woman was waving her arms. "My gold bracelet fell in the water right about there!" she cried, pointing into the water.

Red Trunks was on the dock too. "I'll get it," he cried and jumped into the water. But when he came up, his hands were empty.

Antonio said that he would look for the bracelet too. He put on his mask and fins and climbed down the ladder. He swam out over the spot and dived.

At last Antonio saw the bottom. His mask was clear, and he could see sun spots and shadows on the sand. Here and there were rocks and seaweed. He swam in a slow circle. He was running out of air. Then something flashed in the sun. It was the bracelet! Antonio grabbed it and shot up to the top.

He got fresh air, and the woman got her gold bracelet. Antonio also got his picture in the newspaper over this headline: BOY'S BIG DIVE PAYS OFF. And that's how Antonio learned to become a skin diver.

Checking Comprehension and Skills

1. Where does the story take place? (204)
2. What did Antonio want to do? How did Dave Johnson help Antonio get what he wanted?
3. What were the steps Antonio went through to learn to swim? (208)
4. What kind of person was Antonio? Red Trunks? Dave Johnson? Why do you think as you do?
•5. What is this story all about?
   a. If you go skin diving, you might find a gold bracelet.
   b. A face mask helped Antonio see clearly.
   c. Antonio got over his fear of the water and learned to swim and skin dive.
6. Do you think it is important to learn how to swim? Why do you think as you do?
7. Have you ever taught anyone to do something? What did you teach the person? What steps did you have to go through?

   Which word would you use in this sentence?
○8. There's a high fence that ＿＿ the house.
   fought   surrounds   around

● Story Elements: Main idea
○ Phonics: Vowels (variant sounds)

What Are They?

They live in water all the time. They look a lot like fish, but they are not fish. They have to breathe air above the water because they are mammals. They are strong, large, smart, noisy, and playful.

What are they?

Dolphins and whales!

Using What You Know

You know many ways to enjoy the water. You also know many ways to figure out new words.

Sharpen Your Skills

Here are several ways you've learned to figure out words.

- **Sense and consonants** Think of a word you know that makes sense in the sentence. Then see if the consonants in your word match the consonants in the new word. What words can fit in the sentence below—*duck, boat,* or *dock?*

  The fish swam near the d_ck.

- **Vowels** Sometimes you can't be sure of a word just from using the sense and consonants. Either *duck* or *dock* fits the sentence above. You need to know the vowel letter and the sound it stands for.

  The fish swam near the dock.

- **Syllables** Another way you know to figure out a word is to break it into syllables, figure out the parts, and put the parts together again. Where do you break the underlined words in this sentence?

    My underlined{uncle} says the underlined{river} is so clean that you can see to the underlined{bottom} of it.

- **Meaning** Sometimes you may be able to say a word but still not know what it means. Use the meaning of the words around the unknown word to figure out what it means. Can you figure out what underlined{ruddy} means below?

    Just before the sun set, the sky was red.
    This underlined{ruddy} color was pretty.

Use one or more of these ways to figure out the underlined words below.

Mom, Sue, and I took a short underlined{ramble} around the lake. We like to walk here and there. In one spot, I almost fell down because some of the ground was covered with underlined{slime}. The cool air raised underlined{goosebumps} on Sue's arm. We stood and listened to some birds underlined{chirp}.

Use what you know to figure out words as you read "Tuffy" and "Sea Canaries."

Dionysius and the Dolphin

Many years ago, a boy named Dionysius lived near the sea. He liked to swim with his friends after school.

One day a large dolphin swam into the shallow water where the children were playing. This had never happened before!

1. What do you think the children will do?

The children were frightened and ran out of the water to get away.

The same thing happened several days in a row. But the dolphin never tried to hurt the children. One day Dionysius stayed in the water and touched the dolphin.

After that the dolphin and Dionysius became friends. Every day they would play together. They would swim side by side. Sometimes Dionysius would ride on the dolphin as if it were a horse.

One day as Dionysius was riding on the dolphin, it suddenly turned and swam far out to sea. Dionysius was still on its back!

2. What do you think the dolphin will do with Dionysius? Why do you think so?

Dionysius was not afraid. He knew the dolphin was his friend. He and the dolphin played in the deep water for a while. Then the dolphin brought him back to the shore.

Sharpen Your Skills

As you read, think about what has already happened. Then ask what might happen next.
3. Were your answers to questions 1 and 2 correct? If not, can you find clues that would have helped you to figure out the answers?

In the next two articles, try to figure out what will happen next as you read.

Tuffy, the Navy's Wonderful Dolphin

by Marilyn Sherman

Scientists have found that dolphins can do some surprising things. One is to use sonar to find things in the water. A dolphin sends out little sounds. Then it listens. The sounds bounce back to the dolphin when they hit things in the water. With this sonar, a dolphin can find things even with its eyes covered. A dolphin can also swim faster than any person. It can race a mile[1] in just three minutes.

In the 1960s, the Navy set up a large underwater lab, called Sealab, off the coast of California. It was two hundred feet[2] below the ocean's surface. Scientists could live in it for over a month at a time. They could talk to people on the surface by telephone. But the Navy needed a way to get supplies and mail to the people in Sealab. How could the Navy quickly reach them so far below the surface?

1. 1.6 kilometers
2. 61 meters

The Navy decided to train a dolphin named Tuffy to dive down to Sealab from a pen on the surface. He learned to go to Sealab when a buzzer sounded. When Tuffy heard it, he would carry down mail and supplies in a special bag that he wore.

During his years of working for the Navy, Tuffy had many jobs. His most important job, though, was to save lives.

The people in Sealab often left it to study the ocean's floor. The bottom of the ocean is dark and murky, so they could not see well. They might not be able to find their way back to Sealab. If the people got lost, they would be in danger. They would have only the air in their tanks to breathe.

Since Tuffy had learned to take mail to Sealab, the Navy knew he was smart. They thought they could train him to help lost divers get back to Sealab.

They were right. This is what Tuffy learned to do. First, a lost diver sent a signal that told people in Sealab he was lost. Then someone in Sealab sounded a special buzzer. This was a signal for Tuffy to find the lost diver. Before Tuffy went to the diver, he raced from his pen to Sealab. There he got a line to take to the diver. Only then did Tuffy search for the diver. Tuffy's sonar led him right to the diver, even in the deep, murky waters.

In a flash, the diver had a line to follow back to Sealab. And Tuffy could rush to the surface for his reward—a huge breath of air.

Sea Canaries

by Margery Facklam

Beluga whales are white whales that look a bit like large dolphins. They are sometimes called sea canaries. They live in the cold waters of some oceans and rivers.

There are groups of people who are trying to keep belugas from dying out. These people try to learn as much as they can about the whales. The more they learn, the better they can help them. One day, Heather Malcolm, a young woman working in Toronto, Canada, heard about one group. They would be studying some belugas that lived in a river. Heather wanted to help them. She asked her friend, Leone Pippard, to go with her. At first Leone didn't want to go. Then Leone read a book about a whale that died because no one would help it. That made her decide to go with Heather to study the whales.

Have You Heard?
Belugas are black or dark gray when they are born. They get lighter as they grow. They are white by the time they are five years old.

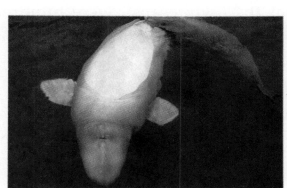

A beluga whale (called a cow) and her baby (called a calf)

It took several months of work to get everything they needed to take. Finally, Leone and Heather borrowed a camper and left for the river. There they would meet the other people who were studying the belugas.

When they got to the river, a cold rain was falling. The fog was so thick they could not find the place where they were to meet the other people.

As Heather and Leone were looking for the meeting place, their camper got stuck in wet sand. It took hard work to dig it out. Bugs bit them so badly that Heather jumped into a dark pool of water to get away from them. She came up covered with slime—the water was polluted. The women didn't find the other people. That night they went to sleep tired and depressed. They wanted to go home!

whitecap, a wave whose top part has been blown into foam by the wind

At dawn the sun shone on waves of **whitecaps** in the river. But how could there be whitecaps when there was no wind? Then they saw that the "whitecaps" were hundreds of belugas coming to the top of the water for air. "It gave us goosebumps," said Heather. "They were so beautiful."

Heather and Leone had a small boat. They rowed it out among the belugas. They were worried because the whales were as long as small trucks. Would the belugas rush at the boat or tip it over? But they only swam beside it, watching the women watching them.

The two women had a wonderful day watching the whales. Later they found the group of people they were to meet. They stayed for several weeks to learn more about the whales.

One day, wearing a diving suit and a face mask, Heather dived in the icy-cold river. She was surprised at the noise under the water as the belugas called to each other. They barked, chirped, clicked, and whistled. "Now I know why they are called sea canaries," she thought. "They sing."

Have You Heard?
Belugas make many different noises. Other kinds of whales make noises also.

Heather and Leone enjoyed their study of the gentle belugas so much that they returned two years later to learn more.

Leone Pippard (left) and Heather Malcolm

Checking Comprehension and Skills

1. When and where does the article about Tuffy take place? (218)

•2. On page 218 you read that the Navy needed a way to reach the people in Sealab. Were you able to figure out that they would use a dolphin? What details helped you figure that out? (218)

3. Are "Tuffy" and "Sea Canaries" fiction or nonfiction? Why do you think as you do?

4. Why are belugas called "sea canaries"? (223)

5. What kind of people are Heather and Leone? Why do you think as you do?

•6. Were you able to figure out that Heather and Leone would stay after they saw the "whitecaps" on the river? What details helped you figure that out? (222)

7. Would you like to have been with Heather and Leone on their trip? Why or why not?

Which word would you use in this sentence?

○8. The ____ in the air made it hard to see.
    lab   fog   frog

• Predicting outcomes
○ Word Study Strategies

Who Would Want To?

FROM # The Deep Dives of Stanley Whale

by Nathaniel Benchley

Reading Bonus

Stanley was a small whale. He was small as whales go because he was still young. But, in fact, he was about as big as a large car.

With his mother and cousins and aunts, Stanley swam through the wide ocean, far from land and people. His father was often away, so Stanley didn't see him much.

When Stanley was very young, he stayed with his mother all the time. But as he got older, he tried doing things for himself. He tried jumping. But he wasn't very good at it. He tried swimming underwater, and he was better at that. But he had to come up for air fairly often, so he couldn't go too deep. Every time he came up, his breath made a big cloud in the air.

Sometimes Stanley's mother would dive down very deep. She would be gone for a long time. When she came up, she would have a lot of fish in her mouth. If she was lucky, she would have a large squid. That was the best eating a whale could find.

Stanley would nibble bits of fish as they fell from her mouth. He wished he could get things like that for himself. Then he could have it all instead of just the pieces.

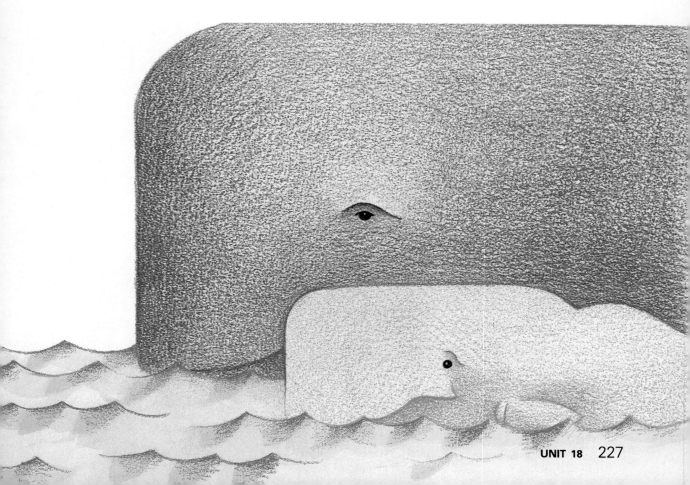

So one day Stanley decided to make a deep
dive on his own. He took three big breaths
and held the last one. Then Stanley flipped
his tail in the air and headed straight down.

He went down and down and down, and
the color of the water changed from light
green to blue to purple to black. Pretty soon
he couldn't see a thing.

Then he saw little sparks of light, which
were shiny fishes. He snapped at one light
and ate it. It tasted good.

"This is the life," he thought. "I'd like to
spend more time down here."

But then his lungs began to hurt, and he
knew he needed air. He started up.

Stanley went up and up and up, and the water changed from black to purple to blue to light green. Just when he thought his lungs were going to burst, he ZOOMED out of the water. Then he fell back with a great splash. His heavy breathing filled the air with clouds.

His mother, who was watching nearby, said, "I thought you'd never get back. How deep did you go?"

"I don't know," Stanley replied, when he could speak. "All I know is it was black."

"That's too deep," she said. "Until you're older, you shouldn't go into the blackness."

"Why not?" said Stanley. "It's fun."

"For one thing, a giant squid might get you," his mother said. "There are some big ones down there that only a grown whale can handle."

"Poof," said Stanley. "I can handle anything."

"You cannot," replied his mother. "And don't go down past the purple."

"Time will tell," said Stanley, thinking it made him sound grown up.

Next day Stanley decided to dive again. His mother saw him getting ready.

"Remember what I told you," she said. "No farther than the purple."

So Stanley went down from the green to the blue to the purple. He swam around looking for things to eat. But there were no fish or squid or anything.

Stanley looked down, where the water was black, and thought he saw all sorts of food. "There is only one thing to do," he told himself. "I have to go down to the black."

Stanley went down slowly, ready to snap at the first thing he saw. But it just got blacker and blacker. And then suddenly, Stanley saw something large and red. Then it changed to white. Then to brown spots.

Stanley drifted deeper to see what it was. By the time he was near the thing, it was red again. Then it was white. Then, suddenly, he realized it was a big squid! It wasn't a giant, but it was big enough. And it was watching him.

Stanley stopped and backed off.

"Looking for something?" the squid asked.

"Just fooling around," said Stanley.

The squid changed to red. "You're either very young or very stupid," it said. "This is no place to be fooling around."

"I wanted to see how you change color," said Stanley. "Is it hard?"

"Not for squids," the squid replied. "But no whales can do it."

"Yes, they can," said Stanley. "I know a whale, and he's all white."

"Can he change?" asked the squid.

"Well, no," said Stanley. "Not exactly."

"Then he's not so smart," said the squid. "He's just like any other whale. Whales annoy me."

Stanley noticed that the squid had been coming closer to him. He edged away.

"Excuse me, it's time for me to breathe," he said.

"Stay around awhile," the squid said, coming closer. "Breathing isn't everything."

"It is for me," said Stanley, and he started up.

The squid shot out two arms and caught him and tried to drag him back. Stanley shouted, "Hey! Cut it out!"

Just then his mother plunged down and snapped off the squid's arms. She turned to get the rest of the squid. But it had gone, leaving only a cloud of black ink behind.

"Come on," said Stanley's mother. "Let's go up." And up they went—through the purple, the blue, and the light green—to daylight.

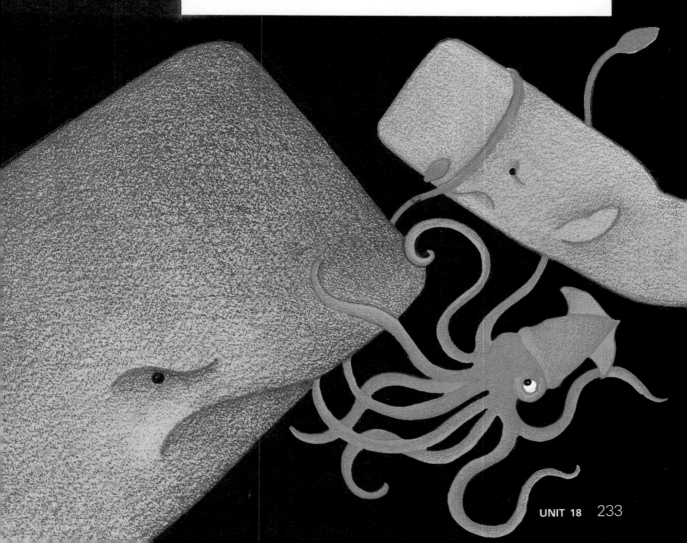

Looking Ahead in Your Reading

Meet Ethel Glug, diver. Ethel likes to take a nice dip in the ocean now and then. There's no telling what she might find— maybe even treasure! But before she dives too far down, Ethel takes a quick look ahead.

Today Ethel's sharp eyes tell her two things. One, check out the ship. Two, stay away from the cave! Do you think looking ahead helps Ethel?

Sharpen Your Skills

When you read, you can learn a lot by looking ahead. Looking ahead is called **previewing.**

You **preview** a book, article, or story by looking it over quickly. You flip pages. You look at titles, pictures, and headings. You see what looks important and what you most want to read.

Preview the selection that begins on this page. Glance at the pictures, title, and other print. Don't try to read every word. Then see if you can answer the questions on page 237.

The Amazing Squid

The squid is one of the most interesting animals under the sea. It looks something like an octopus, but an octopus has only eight arms. A squid has ten.

Squid can be very small or very large. The smallest squid are about two inches[1] long. The biggest can grow to fifty feet.[2] That's bigger than many boats.

When a squid swims, it uses its arms to steer. The suckers on the arms help it hold onto things. A muscle below the head helps it swim.

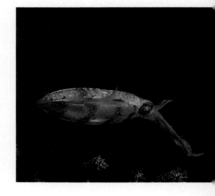

The bodies of some squid glow in deep water.

---

1. 5 centimeters   2. about 15 meters

Parts of a squid's body

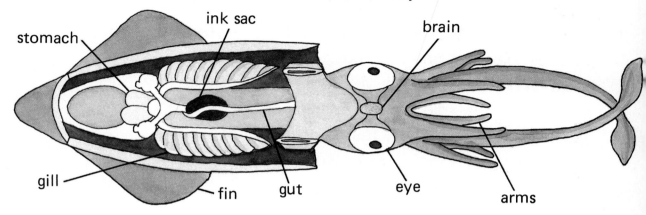

If danger comes, the squid can hide in a cloud of ink. It makes the ink in a "sack" inside its body. It lets ink out when it is afraid. It can also hide by changing its color.

Many people like to eat squid. They think squid taste great. In New England, squid are used as bait to help catch fish.

Squid can be dangerous to people. The large ones have been known to fight humans. The arms of a squid have a strong grip. Squid bite too. Their bodies make a kind of poison. It's never a good idea to tangle with a squid!

Now that you have previewed pages 235 and 236, see what you have learned. Try answering these questions. You can check your answers by turning the page upside down.

1. What is the selection about?
2. Is it a made-up story, or is it an article that gives facts?
3. What can you learn from the pictures?
4. What are some interesting things you might learn from reading the whole selection?

You learned a lot by previewing "The Amazing Squid." Now you can learn even more. Go back and read the whole selection. You'll probably find that your reading goes more quickly and smoothly because you took a look ahead first.

Remember that a preview is a quick look ahead at something you are going to read. By previewing, you can learn what's important and what you most want or need to read.

Answers:
1. It is about squid.
2. It is an article that gives facts.
3. You can learn that the bodies of some squid glow. You can also learn the parts of a squid's body.
4. The answer to this one is up to you. What interests you most?

Books to Read

Kate Heads West by Pat Brisson

Come along with Kate and her best friend, Lucy, on a trip through the West. See cowgirls at a rodeo in Texas. Raft down the Colorado River. Hear millions of bats squeaking in a cave in New Mexico!

Nate the Great and the Musical Note
by Marjorie Weinman Sharmat
and Craig Sharmat

Nate the Great must solve an important case by four o'clock. Musical notes provide the clues. Finding the answer is one thing, Nate learns. Knowing what the answer means is something else.

Stories by Philip Yenawine

Artists often tell stories through their work. Learn how to look for the stories in the paintings and drawings pictured in this book. The author wrote three other books about art—*Shapes, Colors,* and *Lines.* Read them all!

The Choice Is Yours

Maria's Choice

"Guess what, Mom? I don't want to watch TV today," Maria said. "There's nothing worth watching—really. The programs on all the channels are awful. I've decided you're right. If a show is terrible, I shouldn't waste my time watching it. But what is there to do?"

Kids Know What Kids Like

Most kids know what they like to watch on television. So perhaps kids should help decide what kinds of shows go on the air. On one channel, they are doing just that.

Twenty boys and girls between nine and fourteen years old write and star in their own shows. They also handle the sound, lights, and cameras. Other children decide the times at which the shows will go on the air.

Children like different kinds of things. Since this station wants them to watch, it has different kinds of programs. Children can choose to watch plays, cooking shows, news, sports, or other shows. They like watching because other children planned the shows.

A woman is in charge of the station. She must decide which children will do the different kinds of work. She holds tryouts to pick the twenty writers. She looks for young people who like to write and act. In the past, children who were trying out had to write a news story and act in a play.

Children work at this station for a year. Their jobs are the same as those at any TV station. So they learn most of the important things about putting on a TV show.

Sharpen Your Skills

The **cause** is the reason why something happens. The **effect** is what happens. Clue words such as *because, since,* and *so* often help you figure out the cause and effect.

1. Why does the TV channel in the article have different kinds of programs?
2. Why are young people who work there able to learn about regular TV stations?

In the next story find out what happened because a mother turned off her family's TVs.

from
The Week Mom Unplugged the TVs

by Terry Wolfe Phelan

Steve's family owns three TV sets. He and his two sisters watch game shows and cartoons every afternoon. One day his mother says, "Enough!" She decides to unplug all the sets for one whole week.

I couldn't imagine a day without watching TV. And I had to go until Friday at sundown without my shows. It was the worst thing a parent could do to a kid. And I hadn't even done anything wrong. I thought no afternoon snack was bad. But no TV makes an afternoon without a snack look like Easy Street.

Day One

The pulling out of the plugs began on Monday. I invited every friend I had to my house. I needed them so that I could forget what I was missing on TV.

At three o'clock, seven kids arrived. We drank all the milk, ate all the snacks, and used up all the napkins. But Mom only said, smiling, "Glad to have you all here."

When my friends left at five o'clock, all the quiet got to me. I screamed. It didn't do any good. Mom ignored me. My sisters ignored my screaming too.

Then I just sat there in silence. I heard some crickets clicking outside. I had never heard crickets in the afternoon before. I went to the window and looked hard. But no matter how hard I stared, I couldn't see them. So I walked around the house sixteen times and wondered if the cats were still chasing the mice on the 5:30 TV show.

I wrote a letter to my cousin Frank. I asked him if I could visit him. I signed it, "Save me! Your long lost cousin, Steve."

Everyone read that night, except me. I wrote another letter to Frank. It said, "If you don't save me, I'll never be your cousin again."

I went to mail my letters. The crickets' clicks were even louder at night. I wished I could see one of them. After I put my letters in the mailbox, I started home. I noticed a star following me. I ducked behind a bush to hide from that nosy star. It was there waiting when I came out.

Later that first night, I lay in bed and listened to the crickets. I pulled my bed close to the window so I could see that star. And I wondered if the mice got away from the cats on the 5:30 show.

Day Two

Day Two without a TV was almost a rerun of Day One. I didn't invite my friends though. I didn't feel like running out of food again.

I got into bed that night two hours before my usual bedtime. I looked out the window. I couldn't find that nosy star anywhere.

"If I had a telescope I could see it," I thought. I might even see the crickets. A telescope would be like my own TV. I could watch anything I wanted. I could have more than ten channels too. I'll bet there are ten thousand stars I could watch.

I guess I decided right then I would have something to do on Day Three. I would build a telescope.

Day Three

I wanted to start building my telescope.
So the next afternoon I raced home from
school. I didn't even eat anything or read the
TV schedule. I had to get right to work.

I knew telescopes were sort of round, so I
used two cardboard tubes. I took apart my
two magnifying glasses. I used them as
lenses. I put the smaller tube into the larger
one. I used chewing gum to keep the lenses
in place. I was going to have my own TV
again—and in living color.

I painted "on" and "off" knobs on the
tubes to remind me of a regular TV. My
telescope was perfect, except for one thing.
It only had a 1½-inch screen. I didn't care
though. Only my eye had to fit in. And if
the telescope worked right, the pictures would
become ten times their real sizes!

By the time I finished my telescope, it was too dark to see a cricket and too light to see a star. Finally night came. It was so cloudy I couldn't see a thing through my telescope. The only thing left for me to do was to go to bed.

Day Four

By Day Four I had almost forgotten what I was missing on regular TV.

The sun was shining. I grabbed my telescope and ran outside to see my new programs. I noticed a bee on a flower. It was time for an instant replay. I pulled the tubes back and forth in order to focus on the bee. Even I was surprised with how much I saw.

I looked at everything through my telescope. Since I was looking so hard, I even found my lost skate key hanging on a bush. I had been looking for that key ever since the last snow melted. My week was really starting to look up.

It took ages for Day Four to finally get dark. But I was ready when the first star appeared in the sky. I looked through my telescope. The sky shows at night were wonderful.

Just when I was focusing on the moon, my cousin Frank called. He was ready to save me. But I was too busy to be saved. I told him to write me a letter. I would answer it if I had time.

Checking Comprehension and Skills

1. Put these story events in order.
    a. Steve decided to build a telescope.
    b. Steve saw wonderful sky shows at night.
    c. Mom unplugged the TV sets.
    d. Steve screamed because of the quiet.
●2. Why did Steve decide to build a telescope? (247)
3. What steps did he use to build it? (248)
●4. Why do you think Steve's mother decided to unplug the TV sets?
5. When the TV sets are plugged in again at the end of Day Five, how do you think Steve will react? Why do you think as you do?
6. Do you think it was a good idea to unplug the TV sets? Why or why not?
7. What might you learn from having your own TV set unplugged for five days? Why?

Which word would you use in this sentence?
○8. She broke the _____ in her glasses.
    surprised   watches   lenses

● Cause and effect relationships
○ Dictionary: Root word and inflected form

Moving

How do you feel about moving? Do you think of it as a loss—of old friends, familiar places, and favorite things? Or do you think of it as a chance—to make new friends, see new places, and do new things?

No matter how children feel about moving, they may have no choice in the matter. They probably have to move whenever their family decides to move.

The "I-Won't-Forget" Box

Loretta went out and sat on the steps. It was hot in the backyard! It felt strange to her too. Her family had only lived in Oklahoma City for two weeks. The yard and the house still seemed so different from Detroit. She wished she were back there.

Loretta picked up a big box and balanced it on her knees. It was the box her ice skates had come in. When her dad saw her hanging up the skates in her new bedroom closet, he said, "Not much snow and ice here in Oklahoma City." If only he'd told her that *before* they moved, she'd have given her skates to her cousin Ruthie.

Good old Ruthie. Loretta opened the box and found Ruthie's picture.

One by one, Loretta took out some other things that reminded her of home: the ticket from that extra-inning game when the Tigers beat the Yankees, her old library card, and an envelope full of sand from the lake.

Loretta had packed this box of special things to help her remember Detroit. She usually felt better just looking at them and remembering. But today she felt lonely. She wondered what she should do. Maybe that girl down the block, the one about her own age, would like to see the box. And maybe the girl would know if there was any place in Oklahoma City to go ice skating.

Sharpen Your Skills

Sometimes there are no clue words to tell you why something happens. You have to figure out the reasons for yourself.

1. Why did Loretta save the things that were in the box?
2. Why did Loretta think she should have given her ice skates to her cousin?

Think about why the boy doesn't want to move west in the next story.

GILA MONSTERS MEET YOU AT THE AIRPORT

by Marjorie Weinman Sharmat

I live at 165 East 95th Street, New York City, and I'm going to stay here forever.

My mother and father are moving. Out West. They say I have to go too. They say I can't stay here forever.

Out West nobody plays baseball because they are too busy chasing buffaloes. And there's cactus everywhere you look. But if you don't look, you have to stand up just as soon as you sit down.

Out West it takes ten minutes just to say hello. Like this: H–O–W–W–W–D–Y, P–A–A–A–R–R–D–N–E–R.

Out West I'll look silly all the time. I'll have to wear chaps and spurs and a hat so big that nobody can find me under it. And I'll have to ride a horse to school every day, and I don't know how.

Out West everybody grows up to be a sheriff. I want to be a subway driver.

My best friend is Seymour, and we like to eat salami sandwiches together. Out West I probably won't have any friends. If I do, they'll be named Tex or Slim. We'll eat chili and beans for breakfast and lunch and dinner. And I'll miss Seymour and salami.

I'm on my way. Out West. It's cool in the airplane.

The desert is so hot you can collapse, and then the buzzards circle overhead. But no one rescues you because it's real life and not the movies. There are clouds out the window. But there are no buzzards yet.

Seymour says there are Gila monsters and horned toads out West. I read it in a book too. So I know it's so. But Seymour says they meet you at the airport.

We're here. Out West. I don't know what a Gila monster or a horned toad looks like, but I don't think I see any at the airport.

I see a boy in a cowboy hat. He looks like Seymour, but I know his name is Tex. "Hi," I say.

"Hi," he says. "I'm moving East."

"Great!" I say.

"*Great?*" he says. "What's so great about it? Don't you know that the streets are full of gangsters? They all wear flowers in their lapels so they look honest. But they zoom around in big cars with screeching brakes. You have to jump out of their way.

"In the East it snows and blows all the time, except for five minutes when it's spring and summer.

"And you have to live on the 50th floor. Airplanes fly through your bedroom, and you've got to duck fast.

"They ran out of extra space in the East a long time ago. It's so crowded people going to work have to sit on top of each other on the subways.

"And alligators live in the sewers. I read it in a book, so I know it's so."

Then the mother and father of the boy who looks like Seymour but isn't grab his hand, and he goes off. "Sometimes the alligators get out," he yells to me. "And they wait for you at the airport."

It's warm, but there's a nice breeze. We're in a taxi riding to our new house. I don't see any horses yet. I don't see any buffaloes either.

I see a restaurant just like the one in my old neighborhood. I see some kids playing baseball. Finally I see a horse. Hey, that's a great-looking horse!

Here's our house. Some kids are riding their bicycles in front of it. I hope one of them is named Slim.

Tomorrow I'm writing a long letter to Seymour. I'll tell him I'm sending it by pony express. Seymour will believe me. Back East they don't know much about us Westerners.

Checking Comprehension and Skills

•1. Why do you think the boy who is telling the story didn't want to move?

•2. Why do you think he changed his mind about moving and decided to become a Westerner?

3. Do you think it was silly of the boy not to want to move out West? Why or why not?

4. What were some of the things the boy who was moving East thought he would find? Do you think he found them? Why or why not?

5. Which sentence sums up this story?

   a. A boy who was moving West was going to miss salami sandwiches.

   b. A boy was afraid of the West because he didn't know what it was really like.

6. If you had to move, where would you like to move and why? What would you miss most about where you live now?

Which word would you use in each sentence?

○7. The collar and ___ of the coat are blue.
   socks   shoes   lapels

○8. That's the best food I've eaten in a ___!
   restaurant   cactus   breeze

• Cause and effect relationships
○ Dictionary: Pronunciation

Brenda

After You Choose

Making a choice can be hard. You have to think a lot about the problem. Maybe you ask other people what they think. Finally you decide what to do.

Sometimes what happens next is even harder than making the choice. You have to follow through on the choice you made.

Finding the Meaning in a Dictionary

I wrote my cousin a long <u>letter</u>.

Which picture do you think goes with the sentence above? Which kind of *letter* did the girl write?

Sharpen Your Skills

Sometimes when you read you are not sure about the meaning of a word. If that happens, first look at the sentence the word is in. Then look at the sentences before and after. See if that helps you figure out the meaning. If not, look up the word in a dictionary or glossary.

Suppose you looked up the word *letter*. You might find an entry like the one on page 267.

> **let·ter** (let′ər), **1** mark or sign that stands for one of the sounds that make up words. There are 26 letters in our alphabet. **2** mark with letters: *Please letter a new sign.* **3** a written or printed message: *He told me about his vacation in a letter.* 1, 3 *noun,* 2 *verb.*

Sometimes more than one definition of an entry word is given. Find the three definitions of *letter.* Think about how these meanings are different. Notice the sentences in special print after definitions 2 and 3. These sentences show how *letter* can be used with each meaning. You can also see that the parts of speech for the definitions are given at the end of the entry. "1, 3 *noun*" means that definitions 1 and 3 are for nouns.

When more than one meaning is given for a word, read all the meanings. Then choose the one that makes the most sense in the sentence in which the word is used.

1. Which definition of *letter* makes the most sense in the sentence on page 266?
2. Tell which definition makes sense in this sentence: Did you dot the <u>letter</u> *i?*

Use your dictionary to look up words you are not sure of as you read.

Following the Warbler's Song

I am a bird watcher. Friday's newspaper said that a Kirtland's warbler was seen in the woods near my apartment. Since that is a rare kind of bird, I wanted to see it.

Saturday turned out to be cold and misty. But the bird might leave the area. I thought I should try to see it that day.

I got to the woods and started walking. I knew how the warbler sounded, so I whistled its song over and over. I tramped around for about two hours without seeing the bird. My feet became sore, and I was cold and wet from the mist.

Suddenly, I slipped in some mud. I fell and bumped my arm. Now I had a sore arm as well as sore feet. And I was dirty and even more cold and wet.

Just then a warbler answered the song I made. The warbler was nearby! I whistled the song again. The bird answered. It kept answering my song as I slowly crept closer to it. Finally I crept around some bushes. There was another bird watcher. It had been her warbler song answering mine!

Sharpen Your Skills

Sometimes many effects happen because of one cause. Clue words like *since* and *because* may help you find the cause and its effects. Sometimes there are no clue words to help you.

Although it was cold and misty, the girl in this story decided to look for a rare bird.
1. Why did she decide to try to see it?
2. Tell two things that happened to her because of that choice.

Notice what happens to people in the next two stories because of choices they make.

Changing Things for the Better

by Annette Wallen

Many people work hard so that the world will be a better place to live. One of those people is José Treviño. He works to protect wild animals. He also teaches people how important wild animals are to all of us.

José Treviño loves being outside. He also loves animals. So he wanted to study wild animals. He went to school for many years.

With all his years of school, Treviño could get a job with regular hours and good pay. But Treviño works long, hard hours for very little pay. He does this because, as he says, "I want to do something for my country." In fact, he's doing quite a lot.

Treviño works for the government of Mexico. He is in charge of all the wildlife in Chihuahua,[1] the largest state in Mexico. Much of the country in Chihuahua is desert. To some people, the desert may not seem interesting. But to Treviño, it is full of color and beauty.

---

1. Chihuahua (chi wä'wä)

In his job, Treviño does many kinds of work. In some months he must do a lot of driving to do his job. He helps ranch workers find mountain lions that are killing cattle. He makes sure hunters have licenses. He stops people who are breaking wildlife laws. At other times, Treviño works in his office. He studies or has dull paperwork to do. Treviño's studies are important to him. He is studying ways to help antelopes, one of his favorite kinds of animals.

For a long time, Treviño was the only person whose job was looking after the wild animals of Chihuahua. This made his job lonely. Now he has someone to help him. But Chihuahua is so big that Treviño could use a hundred more people to share his work.

Treviño feels that one of his most important jobs is talking to the people of Chihuahua. He knows wild animals are an important part of Mexico's past. So he thinks people should be able to enjoy them in years to come. He tells this to others. He helps them find ways to save wild animals.

Sometimes Treviño must wonder if his choice to help Mexico's wild animals is worth all the hard work. You might think that one person couldn't really make a difference. But Treviño knows that things are changing. People are listening to him. Animals are better protected now. Treviño says what he does is worth hard work. And he enjoys it!

Miracle in Rome

by Betty Millsaps Jones

On September 8, 1960, Wilma Rudolph stood in the Olympic Stadium in Rome, Italy. It takes years of hard work to become an Olympic champion. But for Wilma, being in the Olympics was like a miracle. As a child, she had not been able to walk.

When Wilma was four, she had been very, very sick. Doctors saved her life. But after she got well, Wilma could not move her left leg. The doctors said that she might never walk again. But Wilma's parents gave her lots of love, and they never lost hope. "Wilma *will* walk again," her mother said.

One day each week, Wilma and her mother got up early and rode a bus to a hospital. It was a long, hard trip for them.

Slowly, very slowly, Wilma's leg began to get stronger. When she was six, doctors put a brace on her leg. When Wilma tried to walk, she had to hop.

Two years later, the doctors took the brace off her leg. Wilma limped. But she could walk! For three more years, Wilma had to wear special shoes. Since she had missed being able to run and play before, she wanted to run everywhere now.

Nine years later Wilma was in the 1960 Olympics. She had won gold medals in two races. On September 8, Wilma had a chance to win a third gold medal in the Olympics. Very few people have ever done that.

Wilma and three American teammates would run the 400-meter relay race. In a relay, each runner runs only one part of the race. Wilma would run the last 100 meters.

The starting gun fired. Wilma's first teammate leaped forward. In her hand, she carried a stick called a baton. She had to hand it to the next runner. She ran very fast and took the lead. She passed the baton. Now the second runner on Wilma's team raced down the track.

The third runner grabbed the baton. She sped toward Wilma. She reached out to hand Wilma the baton. Then the crowd gasped because the third runner had nearly dropped the baton.

A runner from Germany ran right past Wilma. Wilma's team had lost its lead!

Wilma made sure that she had the baton in her hand. Then she sped forward.

Years before her mother had told her, "Never give up. Never give up." Wilma remembered. She ran faster and faster. She came closer to the girl from Germany.

Wilma neared the finish line. She leaned forward. The crowd cheered wildly as Wilma crossed the line first. Wilma Rudolph had won her third gold medal!

Checking Comprehension and Skills

1. What is José Treviño's job? (270)
- 2. Why did he choose the job he has? (270)
3. Pretend you have José Treviño's job. What are some things you would like about it? What are some things you would not like?
4. If you could choose to do one thing to help your city or school, what would it be?
5. In what ways are José Treviño and Wilma Rudolph alike?
6. What did Wilma Rudolph and her mother choose? (273)
- 7. In order to walk again, what were some hard things Wilma Rudolph had to do? (273-274)
- 8. When Wilma couldn't walk, her mother told her, "Never give up." How did those words help Wilma in the Olympics? (275)

Which definition of brace in the glossary—the first or the second—goes with each sentence?
o 9. She braced herself for the sad news.
o 10. He walks with a brace on his leg.

- Cause and effect relationships
o Dictionary: Word meaning

Which Meaning Fits?

Tanya was reading her social studies book. She came across the following sentences: "The first stage ran in 1858. It took 24 days, 18 hours, and 26 minutes to go from St. Louis to San Francisco. At that time, it was the quickest way to travel."

Tanya was puzzled. "How can a stage run?" she thought. "The only stages I've seen were in theaters. Maybe there's another kind of stage." She decided to look up *stage* in the dictionary. Turn the page to see the entry Tanya found.

> **stage** (stāj), **1** the raised platform in a theater on which the actors perform. **2** stagecoach, a coach carrying passengers and parcels over a regular route. *noun.*

Sometimes when you look up a word in a dictionary or glossary, you find more than one definition. How many meanings are given for *stage?* When a word has more than one meaning, first read all of the meanings. Then choose the meaning that makes the best sense in the sentence in which the word appears.

Read both definitions for *stage.* Which meaning fits "The first stage ran in 1858"? Yes, the second definition makes better sense. Which meaning was Tanya thinking of at first?

Read the following sentence. Which meaning of *stage* fits the sentence?

The actors almost fell off the <u>stage</u> when the lights went out.

Remember to use a dictionary or glossary if you are not sure of the meaning of a word in your school books—or any book at all.

What Really Happened?

The Empty City

These buildings are in a city in Central America. The city is different from others you might know. This city is empty.

Over one thousand years ago, this was a busy city filled with people. Then, the people disappeared. The buildings fell down and were covered by jungle trees and plants.

Many cities like this one have been discovered in Mexico and Central America. People who study these cities have discovered some things about them. But there are still many mysteries about the cities that no one has been able to solve.

Why Did They Leave?

Long ago, people called the Mayas built a great empire in Mexico and Central America. They built many fine cities. Their buildings were brightly painted and strong. The Mayas knew a lot about numbers and the planets and the stars. The Mayas knew more about these things than other people did. Why, then, did their empire disappear?

About one thousand years ago, the great Mayan cities became empty. Some people believe the Mayas became sick and died. Others believe they did not have enough food to eat and so they moved to new farmlands. One person who has studied the Mayas thinks they believed the world would come to an end. So they just left their cities and went away.

The cities the Mayas left behind were soon covered by vines and grasses. Trees grew in the open places, and in time the trees fell. The painted stones lost their color. The great cities of the Mayas were covered over by the jungle.

Some Mayas still live in Central America and Mexico. They own farms and shops. But they do not know what happened a thousand years ago. The cities hidden in the jungle are as strange to them as they are to us.

Sharpen Your Skills

Details, or small pieces of information, help you picture what the article is about. Picturing details can help you understand the article.

1. What details told you that the Mayas were once powerful and important?
2. Picture the empty Mayan cities in the jungle. What details do you see?

The details in the next article will help you feel what it must have been like to discover the secret of Palenque.

The Secret of Palenque

by Alan Bickley

This tells about a Mayan city in Mexico that was covered by the jungle and then was found. We call the city Palenque[1] because that is the name of the village nearest to it. But no one knows what the Mayan builders of the city called it. The Mayas left this beautiful city almost one thousand years ago, and no one knows why.

The Discovery of Palenque

After the Mayas left Palenque, few people knew it was there. Native Americans who lived in other parts of the jungle may have known about the old city. But two young boys were the first to tell others about it. They discovered the city in 1746 when they were visiting their uncle in the nearby village.

As years went by, **archaeologists** began to visit Palenque. They wanted to find out what Palenque looked like when it was a great

archaeologists, scientists who study the cities and people of long ago

---

1. Palenque (pä len′kā)

city. They pulled the jungle plants away from the buildings. They dug under the dirt to find other buildings.

Alberto Ruz Lhullier

An archaeologist named Alberto Ruz Lhullier[1] made a great discovery at Palenque. He had begun to **restore** some of the buildings there in 1949.

restore, to bring back to an earlier appearance

---

1. Alberto Ruz Lhullier (äl ber'tō rüs lü lē ā')

In this building, Ruz made a great discovery.

While he was working inside one of them, he saw some large stone slabs set in the floor. In the slabs were finger holes. The slabs were very heavy, but with the help of other men, he lifted them. Under them was a stairway stretching farther than he could see. He had to know what was down there!

The Stairway

The long stairway was filled with dirt. Ruz and his men had to dig the dirt out before they could get to the end of it. All the digging had to be done by hand with small tools. The dirt had to be carried up in buckets. There wasn't much air to breathe, and the men became sick.

Ruz was born in 1906. He studied in Mexico, worked for the government, and was an archaeologist for the university in Mexico City. He died in 1979.

The work was slow. And when the rainy time of the year came, the dirt turned to mud. The men could not work at all.

When the rainy time of the year was over, they started digging again. This went on for four years. The men had no idea what they would find.

Then, they came to the end of the stairway. They had dug seventy feet[1] down into the ground. In front of them stood a stone wall. Some people might have given up. Ruz and his men did not.

---

1. about 21 meters

Digging the dirt out of the stairway was hard work.

Behind the Wall

Alberto Ruz Lhullier was not going to be stopped by a wall of stone. He was sure that something wonderful would be found on the other side of that wall.

Working with great care, Ruz's men took down the wall. They found a small room. On the other side of the room was another stone door. In front of the door was a stone box. They lifted the lid off the box. Inside was a treasure of jewels and other things put there over a thousand years before.

A treasure of jewels was found in a small room.

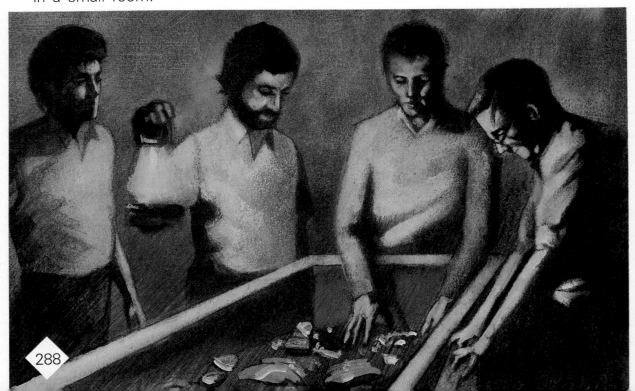

Ruz was almost sure that he would find more jewels on the other side of the next wall. But when the wall was broken, he found, not jewels, but the bones of six people. Ruz guessed that the people had been chosen to stay there to watch over the tomb of a Mayan ruler.

vault, a place of burial

The Treasure

More digging brought Ruz and his men to another room. In it was a large **vault.** Ruz's guess was right. Inside the vault were the bones of a person who must have been a very important Maya. The bones were covered with beautiful jewels and many jade carvings. A jade mask was also in the vault.

One of the jade carvings showed who the man was. He was Lord Pacal,[1] who ruled the Mayas for over sixty years.

Some years later the vault and everything in it were moved to the National Museum in Mexico City. You can see it there today.

This huge carved stone covered the vault.

---

1. Pacal (pä käl')

Visiting the Tomb

If you are in Palenque, you can visit the building where Ruz made his great discovery. You can follow the passage dug by Ruz and his men to the tomb of Lord Pacal.

Discovering the hidden tomb took Ruz and his men four years. Walking through the passage today takes less than one hour.

The Mayas are gone from Palenque, but they have left many secrets behind. Discovering them will be hard and dangerous. But Alberto Ruz Lhullier would have said that it is work well worth doing.

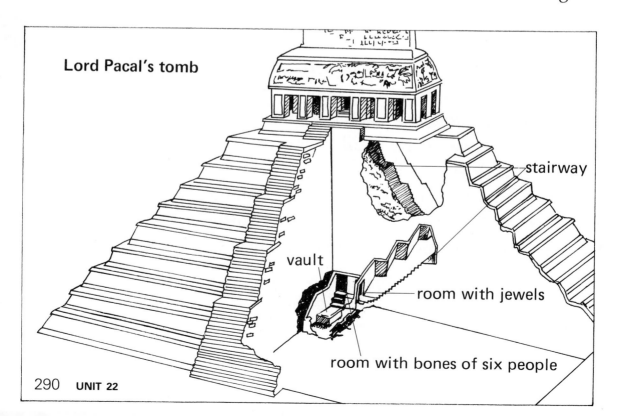

Lord Pacal's tomb

stairway

vault

room with jewels

room with bones of six people

Checking Comprehension and Skills

- 1. Who built Palenque? (284)
  2. Why did archaeologists go to Palenque? (284)
  3. Who was Alberto Ruz Lhullier and what did he discover?
  4. What kind of person was Ruz?
- 5. What details helped you picture Ruz and his men digging out the stairway? (286–287)
- 6. What details helped you picture the first room that Ruz found? (288)
  7. How do you think Ruz felt when he saw what was in Lord Pacal's tomb?
  8. Would you have liked to work with Ruz and his men? Why or why not?

  Which word would you use in each sentence?
- ○ 9. The jade ____ were beautiful.

     carvings   canals   careful
- ○10. He had been a good king for ____ years.

     silky   sixty   sickly

●Details
○Context and consonants

Codes

The two girls in this picture have received a secret message. It is written in code. A code is a special language. In a code, numbers, pictures, or silly words stand for other letters or words.

The girls are trying to "break" the code. They want to find out which numbers stand for which letters. When they do, they will have the key to the code. Then they will know what the message is.

Figuring Out the Meaning That Makes Sense

▲∴ ▲⊙■■ ∧●∴━⋯ ▫▼∴⊙● ~/∶∴ ◆//★

WE WILL BREAK THEIR CODE SOON .

Sal changed the secret message back into English. She showed it to Patty, but Patty didn't get the message. "How could anyone *break* a code?" Patty asked. "It's not a machine or a toy—it's words!"

Sharpen Your Skills

Patty didn't know that the word *break* has more than one meaning. It can mean "damage." But *break* can also mean "make known." To break a code is to make its secret known.

Read the tips on the next page to help you figure out the right meaning for any word that has more than one meaning.

- Look at the other words around the word. Figure out which meaning of the word makes the best sense in the sentence.
- Keep reading to see if that meaning is the right one.
- If it is not, go back and read again. Look for more clues to the right meaning.
- If you need to, use the dictionary to find the meaning that makes the best sense.

Now figure out the meaning that makes sense for each underlined word.

1. The secret message said the gold was in a metal box in the old bank.
2. A band of gold miners took all their gold there long ago.
3. To take the gold out, you had to know how to open the catch on the lid of the box.

Use the tips to help you decide what some words mean as you read the following selections.

Secret Plans

    Sarah and Paul sat on the back porch. Sarah had been thinking for two days about how to surprise their sister, Marsha, on her birthday. It was hard to keep a secret from Marsha. She always found clues that helped her guess what was going on. But Sarah wasn't going to give up!

    "This time Marsha's party is going to be a real surprise," said Sarah. "This time we will send out invitations in code."

    "What do you mean?" asked Paul.

    "I'll write down the alphabet here. Then I'll put a number below each letter like this."

A B C D E F G H I J K L M N O P Q R
1 2 3 4 5 6 7 8 9 10 11 12 13 14 15 16 17 18

S T U V W X Y Z
19 20 21 22 23 24 25 26

"I see," said Paul. "We write numbers instead of letters!"

"Or letters instead of numbers," said Sarah. "Let's hope she won't break our code."

Late at night Marsha sneaked into Sarah's room. She found the birthday code. She saw:

16–1–18–20–25   1–20   B   15–14

19–1–20–21–18–4–1–25

Do you know when the party will be?

Sharpen Your Skills

When you read, you can figure out things by yourself. You can understand more about people and events in a story by thinking about the details the writer gives you.

1. What details tell you the kind of person Sarah is?
2. Is Marsha a good detective? What details tell you that?

The details in the next two articles will help you understand who Thomas Beale was and why he did what he did.

The Treasure of Thomas Beale

by Karen Parker

Thomas Jefferson Beale[1] lived more than one hundred years ago. He lived a life of adventure and mystery, but not much is known about him. We do know that he left a great treasure that no one has been able to find.

Beale was born in Virginia. When he was about thirty years old, he went out west with some other men. Some place north of Santa Fe,[2] New Mexico, they found gold.

The men settled down to mine the gold. As they worked, they also found silver. When

---

1. Beale (bēl)
2. Santa Fe (san'tə fā')

they had several thousand pounds of gold and silver, Beale and a few others went back to Virginia. They hid the treasure there and then returned west. Two years later they made another trip back to Virginia with even more gold and silver.

Beale lived a dangerous life. He knew that the secret of where the treasure was buried would be lost if he and the other men were killed. So before Beale left Virginia for the last time, he put papers telling about the treasure in a locked box. He gave the locked box to his friend Robert Morriss.

Later, Morriss got a letter from Beale. The letter told Morriss to open the box after ten years. It said Morriss would find some papers in the box. The papers were written in different codes. They would mean nothing to anyone without the keys to solve the codes. Beale planned to send Morriss the keys to the codes in another letter.

But Morriss never heard from Beale again. In fact, Morriss forgot about Beale and the box. Morriss didn't open the box until twenty years after he received it. When he did, he found a letter telling him that Beale had found a great treasure and hidden it. Morriss also found other papers covered with numbers.

These papers meant nothing to Morriss. He had never received the keys for the codes. He never knew where Beale's treasure was hidden.

A Fortune for the Finding

by John Alvarez

There are many tales of lost treasure. Some are just made-up stories to be told around a campfire. But the story of Thomas Beale and his fortune is different. It really happened.

Thomas Beale hid a treasure of gold and silver someplace in Virginia. He left three codes telling about the treasure with a friend, Robert Morriss.

Code Number One told exactly where the treasure was hidden. Code Number Two told what the treasure was. Code Number Three told who was to get the treasure.

This is Code Number One. It tells where the treasure is hidden. Can you break it?

71, 194, 38, 1701, 89, 76, 11, 83, 1629, 48, 94, 63, 132, 16, 111, 95, 84, 341, 975, 14, 40, 64, 27, 81, 139, 213, 63, 90, 1120, 8, 15, 3, 126, 2018, 40, 74, 758, 485, 604, 230, 436, 664, 582, 150, 251, 284, 308, 231, 124, 211, 486, 225, 401, 370, 11, 101, 305, 139, 189, 17, 33, 88, 208, 193, 145, 1, 94, 73, 416, 918, 263, 28, 500, 538, 356, 117, 136, 219, 27, 176, 130, 10, 460, 25, 485, 18, 436, 65, 84, 200, 283, 118, 320, 138, 36, 416, 280, 15, 71, 224, 961, 44, 16, 401, 39, 88, 61, 304, 12, 21, 24, 283, 134, 92, 63, 246, 486, 682, 7, 219, 184, 360, 780, 18, 64, 463, 474, 131, 160, 79, 73, 440, 95, 18, 64, 581, 34, 69, 128, 367, 460, 17, 81, 12, 103, 820, 62, 116, 97, 103, 862, 70, 60, 1317, 471, 540, 208, 121, 890, 346, 36, 150, 59, 568, 614, 13, 120, 63, 219, 812, 2160, 1780, 99, 35, 18, 21, 136, 872, 15, 28, 170, 88, 4, 30, 44, 112, 18, 147, 436, 195, 320, 37, 122, 113, 6, 140, 8, 120, 305, 42, 58, 461, 44, 106, 301, 13, 408, 680, 93, 86, 116, 530, 82, 568, 9, 102, 38, 416, 89, 71, 216, 728, 965, 818, 2, 38, 121, 195, 14, 326, 148, 234, 18, 55, 131, 234, 361, 824, 5, 81, 623, 48, 961, 19, 26, 33, 10, 1101, 365, 92, 88, 181, 275, 346, 201, 206, 86, 36, 219, 320, 829, 840, 68, 326, 19, 48, 122, 85, 216, 284, 919, 861, 326, 985, 233, 64, 68, 232, 431, 960, 50, 29, 81, 216, 321, 603, 14, 612, 81, 360, 36, 51, 62, 194, 78, 60, 200, 314, 676, 112, 4, 28, 18, 61, 136, 247, 819, 921, 1060, 464, 895, 10, 6, 66, 119, 38, 41, 49, 602, 423, 962, 302, 294, 875, 78, 14, 23, 111, 109, 62, 31, 501, 823, 216, 280, 34, 24, 150, 1000, 162, 286, 19, 21, 17, 340, 19, 242, 31, 86, 234, 140, 607, 115, 33, 191, 67, 104, 86, 52, 88, 16, 80, 121, 67, 95, 122, 216, 548, 96, 11, 201, 77, 364, 218, 65, 667, 890, 236, 154, 211, 10, 98, 34, 119, 56, 216, 119, 71, 218, 1164, 1496, 1817, 51, 39, 210, 36, 3, 19, 540, 232, 22, 141, 617, 84, 290, 80, 46, 207, 411, 150, 29, 38, 46, 172, 85, 194, 36, 261, 543, 897, 624, 18, 212, 416, 127, 931, 19, 4, 63, 96, 12, 101, 418, 16, 140, 230, 460, 538, 19, 27, 88, 612, 1431, 90, 716, 275, 74, 83, 11, 426, 89, 72, 84, 1300, 1706, 814, 221, 132, 40, 102, 34, 858, 975, 1101, 84, 16, 79, 23, 16, 81, 122, 324, 403, 912, 227, 936, 447, 55, 86, 34, 43, 212, 107, 96, 314, 264, 1065, 323, 428, 601, 203, 124, 95, 216, 814, 2906, 654, 820, 2, 301, 112, 176, 213, 71, 87, 96, 202, 35, 10, 2, 41, 17, 84, 221, 736, 820, 214, 11, 60, 760.

Morriss had no luck in breaking the codes. A year before he died, he gave the papers to James Ward, an old friend. Ward tried to break the codes. He finally broke Code Number Two.

Code Number Two told Ward that the treasure was thousands of pounds of gold and silver. Today, the Beale treasure is worth over twenty million dollars.

After working on the codes for twenty years, Ward had no more money. In 1885 he wrote a book called *The Beale Papers*. It told about the treasure and about Beale's codes. Most of the copies of Ward's books were lost in a fire. But there were enough copies left to inspire other treasure hunters. Since Ward's one lucky break, the other two codes have not been broken.

Many people today think they have found the key to Code Number One, telling where the treasure is hidden. When they do, they go to the Blue Ridge Mountains and begin digging. So far everyone has misread the code. No one has found the treasure. But people have dug up a 1930s car and a ninety-pound[1] piece of iron. Both were fun to find, but they were not worth much money.

---

1. almost 41 kilograms

What should you do if you're bitten by the Beale bug? Before you head for the Blue Ridge Mountains, try breaking the codes. The Beale papers are in the public library in Roanoke,[1] Virginia. Who knows? You may be the lucky one to find the fortune.

---

1. Roanoke (rō'ə nōk)

Is the treasure in these hills? No one knows.

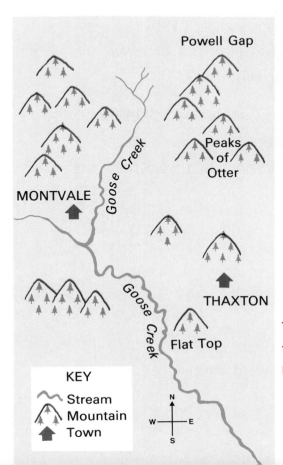

Thomas Beale's treasure may be in this part of the Blue Ridge Mountains, near Roanoke, Virginia.

Checking Comprehension and Skills

1. What did Beale find in New Mexico? (298)
2. Beale wrote codes about the treasure. Why?
•3. What kind of person do you think Beale was? What details tell you that?
•4. Do you think Robert Morriss was a good friend to Thomas Beale? Why or why not?
5. Who was James Ward? (302)
•6. Do you think Thomas Beale changed Ward's life? If so, in what way? (302)
7. Do you think the selections you have just read were fiction or nonfiction? Why?
8. Do you think Code Number One will ever be broken? Why or why not?

Use the following sentence to tell what the underlined word means.

o9. Joan broke the code that told where the treasure is.
   a. smashed
   b. figured out

•Drawing conclusions
oContext: Appropriate word meaning

How to Write a Secret Message

Here is a code you can use to send a message to a friend.

1. Cut small rectangles out of different places on a piece of paper to make a pattern.

2. To make a second pattern, get another piece of paper. Put the pattern over the new paper and draw the rectangles. Then cut them out. Give one of the patterns to a friend.

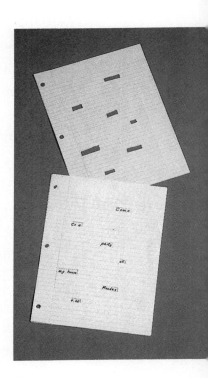

3. Put your pattern over a clean sheet of paper. Write your secret message in the holes.

4. Take the pattern off the paper. Write a letter or a story or just put in any words to fill up the page.

5. Give the paper to your friend. Your friend will put his or her pattern over the paper and will be able to read your message.

UFOS

Almost forty years ago, a pilot in his plane saw nine flat, saucerlike objects racing across the sky. Newspaper writers who heard what happened called the objects "flying saucers." People who read about them thought they were from outer space.

Today, we call any strange object in the sky an "unidentified flying object," or a UFO. Almost all UFOs can be explained. No scientist has yet found one bringing life from outer space. But people still report seeing things in the sky that are never identified.

A Word of Welcome

Quark was a gentle creature who loved visiting Earth in his small spaceship. He liked to collect the strange things he found on Earth. He hardly ever showed himself to Earth people. They became very afraid whenever they saw his huge, red, jellylike body moving toward them.

So when Quark landed in Julio Diaz's yard during a picnic lunch, he wondered how everyone would act. Everyone sat very still, except for Julio who yelled, "Oh, gross!"

Julio's loud voice frightened Quark. Julio's sister Rosa got up, grabbed a small jar from the table, and walked toward Quark.

1. What do you think Rosa will do?

"Here," she said, smiling. "Take it." Quark looked at the jar. In it was something very smooth, shiny, and red.

2. Do you think Quark will take the jar?

The jelly in the jar shook when he touched it. It was beautiful!

Quark shot out two arms and grabbed the jar. He quickly got into his spaceship and shot up through a cloud.

Once safely away he wrote in a notebook: "Gross—a word of welcome."

Sharpen Your Skills

When you read a story, try to predict what will happen next. To **predict** means to figure out what will happen based on what has already happened. As you read, you will find out if your prediction is correct. Your **prediction** is what you said would happen.

3. Did you answer questions 1 and 2 correctly? If not, what details could have helped you make correct predictions?

As you read the next story, try to predict what Bobby and Carol will do when they face an unidentified flying object.

A Simple Explanation

by M. Highsmith

Bobby opened the kitchen door and walked out into the backyard. The evening was warm.

His mom and dad had gone to a meeting. Bobby and his sister, Carol, were supposed to do the dishes. Bobby had washed the dishes, but now he was waiting for his sister to dry them.

"Hurry up, Carol," he called. "I want to play ball before it gets too dark."

The sun was setting. The last rays hit the tops of the trees on the far side of the cornfield. Suddenly, Bobby saw something. Behind the treetops something was moving—fast.

Then, from behind the trees, a huge round shape with an orange glow appeared.

"Carol!" Bobby cried as she came out the door. "Look!"

Carol saw it. The huge orange thing rose again. Then it fell behind the trees.

"What was that!" cried Bobby.

"It must have landed in the pasture," Carol said. "Come on!"

They ran through the vegetable garden, over the fence, across the cornfield, and into the woods. It was dark among the trees. They stopped, out of breath and afraid.

"Maybe it's a . . . you know," said Bobby.

"A UFO?" said Carol. "A spaceship?" She noticed she was shaking. She took a deep breath. "I don't care. I've got to see it."

"Me too," said Bobby.

They went through the woods until they came to the pasture. The pasture was dark. They could just see a large shape and something moving. Then just as their eyes got used to the dark—

A roar! A flash of fire! Suddenly, there was a creature in a silver suit and helmet!

Carol and Bobby screamed. The creature turned toward them. But they were already running, crashing back through the woods, racing across the cornfield, over the fence, through the vegetables, and into the house.

When their hearts stopped pounding, they looked out the window. But they saw nothing and were glad of it.

The next morning Carol, Bobby, and their parents searched the pasture. But they found nothing. Their mom and dad wanted to call the police, but Bobby and Carol asked them not to. The children didn't want people making fun of them.

"Besides," said Carol to Bobby later, "there may be a simple explanation. Let's think about what we know."

It had been round, they decided, and about as big as the garage. They weren't sure about the color. It may have been the setting sun that gave it that orange glow.

"A flying saucer," said Bobby.

"What about that creature?" said Carol. "It wore something strange."

"A spacesuit," said Bobby. "The fire was the engines starting up."

"It made me think of Dad when he's welding," said Carol. "He wears coveralls and a face mask. His welding torch goes WHOOSH when the flames come out."

"Dad was not welding in the pasture last night," said Bobby.

"What I mean is," said Carol, "lots of things make a roaring fire. And all kinds of people wear coveralls and helmets."

"Like football players from Mars," said Bobby.

Carol ignored him. "What," she asked herself, "is round, floats through the air, and carries a person in a suit and helmet?"

That afternoon, when Carol was looking through the newspaper, something caught her eye. Each Sunday there was something different at the fairground—a horse show, a dance, a race. And this Sunday—

"That's it!" she cried. She got Bobby and they rode their bikes to the fairground. She didn't tell him why, but when they got there, he knew.

Eight hot-air balloons were being given a preflight check before a race. Some were still flat on the ground. Some were being filled with air from huge fans. Others were having their air heated to make them rise. The air was heated with burners that flamed and roared.

"Look," said Carol. She pointed to a man in silver-gray coveralls. He carried a helmet. She and Bobby ran over to him and said, "Hello."

"Hi," he said. Then he looked at them closely. "Say, last night I came down in a pasture by mistake. Aren't you the two kids who scared me?"

"*We* scared *you?*" asked Bobby. Then he and Carol began to laugh. They remembered themselves crashing through the woods and corn, falling over the fence, and tearing through the garden.

Checking Comprehension and Skills

1. At what time of day did Bobby and Carol see the strange object in the pasture? (310)
• 2. Could you predict how Bobby and Carol would act when they first saw the thing? What details helped you? (311)
3. How do you think they would have acted if they had seen the thing during the day?
4. Do you think Bobby hoped the thing would really be a UFO? Why do you think that?
• 5. Could you predict that Carol would find an explanation for what they saw in the pasture? What details helped you?
6. How did the newspaper story help Carol? (315)
7. What was really in the pasture? (315–316)
8. What kind of person is Carol?

Which definition of weld in the glossary—the first or the second—goes with each sentence?
○ 9. Wanting to find out what they had seen welded Bobby and Carol together.
○10. The workers welded the pieces of metal.
○11. Our work welded us into good friends.

•Predicting outcomes
○Dictionary: Word meaning

Stop and Check

If you saw one of the objects in the picture, would you call it a flying saucer? Or would you be like Carol in the story you just read? Would you stop and check to see if another explanation made sense?

Sometimes when you read, you might start to get mixed up. That's a good time to stop and check yourself. Ask yourself some questions:

- I know reading has to make sense. Does this make sense? Do I understand what it is about?
- Would it help to read some parts again?
- Are there any words I don't know? Should I go back and try to figure them out?

You can help yourself when you read. Stop and check to see if things make sense!

Section Nine

Go for It!

When You Go for It

Not much was known about Colorado in 1806. An American named Pike was sent to explore there. Pike found many places and learned many things. One place he learned about was this mountain. It has been named for him—Pikes Peak.

Many places are named for the people who find them or study them. Cities, states, and even countries may be named to honor people.

Honors are often given to people who "go for it."

Her Name Is on the Map

Francisca Benicia de Vallejo[1] lived in California in the 1800s. And to prove it, her name is on the map.

Francisca was born in San Diego. At that time, California was owned by Mexico. When Francisca was old enough, she married a man who was in the Mexican army. They moved to an army post on San Francisco Bay. Two years later they moved to Sonoma, their home for the rest of their lives.

Francisca's husband was going to start a city on the edge of San Francisco Bay. The city was to be named "Francisca" in her honor. However, another city had grown near the Mexican army post. People wanted to name that city "San Francisco." A nearby city named "Francisca" would have been confusing. So the new city was named "Benicia" instead. Since it has Francisca's middle name, the city is named in her honor anyway!

Another nearby city, Vallejo,[2] is also named in honor of Francisca Vallejo's family.

---

1. Francisca Benicia de Vallejo (frän sēs'kä bā nē'syä dā bī yä'hō   2. Vallejo (və lä'hō)

Sharpen Your Skills

Using a map is one way to find out where places are. The **arrows** show which way is north, south, east, or west. The **scale** can help you figure out how far it is between two places.

1. In which direction would Francisca have gone if she went from her home in Sonoma to Benicia?

2. About how far is Benicia from San Francisco?

The map on page 326 will help you follow the trip of a group who explored the American West.

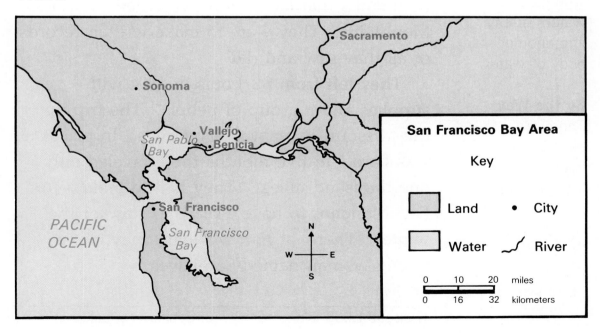

Sacramento

Sonoma

Vallejo
San Pablo
Bay
Benicia

San Francisco Bay Area

Key

San Francisco

PACIFIC
OCEAN

San Francisco
Bay

Land   • City

Water   River

N
W — E
S

| 0 | 10 | 20 | miles |
| 0 | 16 | 32 | kilometers |

A Trip to Remember

by Jackson Harper

The Expedition

The United States was a young country in 1803. Little was known about its huge western lands. But in that year, two army officers named Meriwether Lewis and William Clark were ordered to explore that area. They were to travel from the **mouth** of the Missouri River to the Pacific Ocean. They were to find the safest and easiest way through the high mountains that later would be called the Rocky Mountains. They were to make written records of all they saw and did.

They left from St. Louis in 1804 with supplies and a group of people. The trip up the Missouri River was dangerous. In places it was hard. In five months they traveled only one thousand miles.[1] They had to build a fort, Fort Mandan, to have a place to stay for the winter. There, at Fort Mandan, they met a young woman named Sacajawea.[2]

mouth, the end of a river, where its waters empty into another body of water

By the Way
There are several different ways to spell Sacajawea's name, including Sacagawea and Sakakawea. It probably meant "Bird Woman."

---

1. about 1,600 kilometers   2. Sacajawea (sak'ə jə wē'ə)

Sacajawea

Sacajawea had been born in the mountains far to the west. Her people were the Shoshoni.[1] Sacajawea was twelve years old when she and another girl were stolen by enemy Indians. The other girl escaped. But Sacajawea had to stay among the strangers as a slave. She wanted nothing more than to return to her old home and her friends.

She left the Indians that had stolen her when she married a trader. She never gave up her dream of seeing her old home. When she was sixteen years old, she met the men who could help make her dream come true.

Sacajawea

Lewis and Clark knew nothing of the rivers and mountains to the west. They needed guides who knew both the land and the languages of the people who lived there. Sacajawea knew the languages of the people who lived in the mountains. Her husband knew the languages of some of the people who lived along the river. And so it happened that Sacajawea, her husband, and their baby joined Lewis and Clark's expedition.

---

1. Shoshoni (shō shō′nē)

By the Way
Strapping, or tying, a baby to her back left an Indian mother's hands free to work.

The winter of 1804 brought deep snow and bitter cold. The explorers stayed beside the frozen river in the log huts of Fort Mandan. Then, as the spring sun melted the ice, the boats were loaded again. Sacajawea sat in the front of one boat. Her baby was strapped to her back. Her job was to watch for the big rocks and tree limbs under the water that could smash a boat or turn it over.

Sacajawea must have felt excited as the boats pulled away from shore. She did not know all that lay ahead. But she knew that she was free and that she was going home.

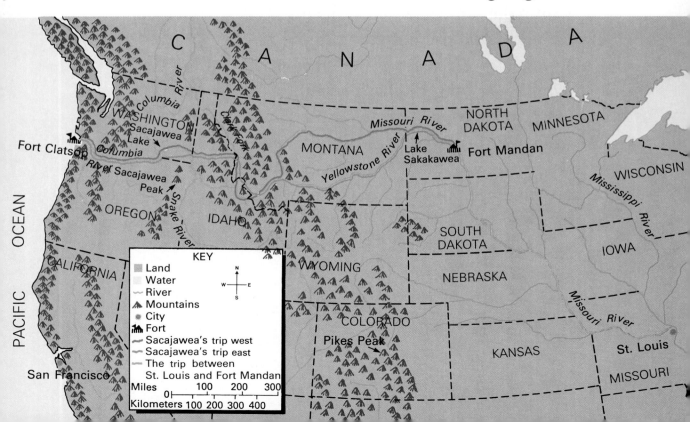

KEY

- Land
- Water
- ～ River
- ⛰ Mountains
- City
- 🏛 Fort
- ━ Sacajawea's trip west
- ━ Sacajawea's trip east
- ━ The trip between St. Louis and Fort Mandan

Miles 0 100 200 300
Kilometers 100 200 300 400

People on the Expedition

Each person who traveled with Lewis and Clark had special skills. Some were good hunters, and they made sure there was food to eat. Some were fine builders, and they made tents and boats of bark and animal skins. One man, named York, made friends very easily with the people they met. York also knew how to care for the sick. When Sacajawea's baby was very sick, York helped save the baby's life.

York helped to take care of Sacajawea's sick baby.

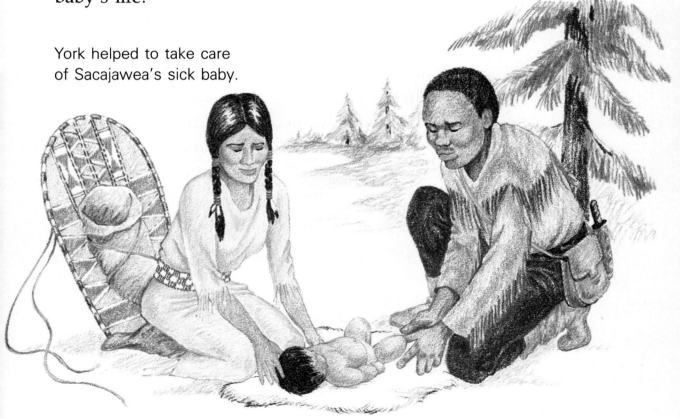

Some of the people on the expedition were good writers. Every day they wrote about what had happened. They made notes about plants and animals they had never seen before. They described the land they saw and the people they met.

From the Mountains to the Ocean

When the expedition came to the mountains, Lewis and Clark began to learn how lucky they were that Sacajawea was with them. Lewis had to decide which paths to take through the mountains. Sacajawea knew the right ones. She also knew there was no river that would take them through the mountains. They would need horses. And her people, the Shoshoni, had more horses than anyone else did.

One day Sacajawea saw a hill that she had seen as a child. She knew then that she was near her home. Soon she saw people she remembered. One was her brother, who was now the chief of the Shoshoni. She was so glad to be home that tears fell from her eyes.

Speaking for Lewis and Clark, Sacajawea asked for horses and guides. The Shoshoni sold them the horses that were needed. Some

Shoshonis went along as guides. A few days later, with Sacajawea pointing the way, the explorers set out again. Never had they seen mountains so rough, forests so deep, or rivers so wild. This was both the hardest and the most beautiful part of their trip.

Seven months after Sacajawea joined the expedition, she saw the Pacific Ocean for the first time. She held her baby high so that he could see it. She stood on the shore watching the shining water for hours.

After the Expedition

The Lewis and Clark expedition ended in September, 1806. When the people returned to the places where they had started, they were heroes. They had done something that no one had done before.

Sacajawea never forgot that great expedition. She remembered the rivers and the mountains, their dangers and their beauty. Most of all she remembered the Pacific Ocean, which she never saw again. Today, almost two hundred years after her trip, we still remember Sacajawea with pride and affection.

Sacajawea was amazed to see so much water.

By the Way
A mountain, two lakes, and many parks have been named to honor Sacajawea.
(See the map on page 326.)

Checking Comprehension and Skills

1. What were the expedition's goals? (324)
•2. If Fort Mandan were still standing, in which state would you find it? (326)
3. Why was it lucky that Sacajawea was on the expedition? (328)
4. Why was York a good person to have on the expedition? (327)
•5. If the explorers could have gone straight from St. Louis to the Pacific Ocean, about how many miles would they have gone? (326)
6. Why do you think places have been named to honor Sacajawea?
7. Would you like to have been with Sacajawea on the expedition? Why or why not?

○8. Choose the spelling change, if any, that was made to the root word of these words when an ending was added.

a. heroes
b. shining

1. drop final *e*
2. double final consonant
3. change final *y* to *i*
4. no spelling change

● Graphic Aids: Maps
○ Structure: Root words with and without spelling changes

Make Your Own Obstacle Course

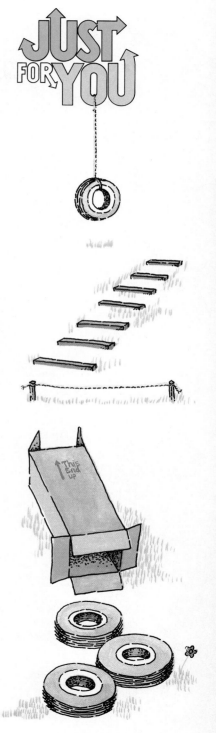

Sacajawea faced many obstacles on her trip. But obstacles can also be fun!

Where can you climb on, crawl under, run through, and jump over obstacles? Yes, on an obstacle course.

You can make an obstacle course in almost any place and with almost anything. Here are some ideas:

Use	To
old tires	jump in and over
pieces of rope	jump rope, jump over
large cartons	crawl through
pieces of wood	make a "ladder"

When you go through the obstacle course, keep track of your time. Each time you go through, try to finish in less time.

Every now and then, change the obstacles. Most of all, have fun!

from
Truly My Own

by Vanessa Howard

I think if I searched a thousand lands
and twice the number in rainbows,
I'd never find one human being
who chose the things that I chose
a person who wanted the things I wanted
or sought what I sought to be

Reading a Schedule

Do you have a favorite TV show? If you do, you probably don't want to miss a minute of it. So you check the TV listings to be sure when the show starts.

Sharpen Your Skills

TV listings are one kind of schedule. A **schedule** is a list of events and when they take place. Trains and buses have schedules too. You'll find schedules in many things you read.

The schedule on the next page shows how a girl who is in a TV show spends the day. How is Sara's day different from yours?

Sara Strong's Day

Time	Activity
7:00 A.M.– 8:00 A.M.	Put on makeup
8:00 A.M.–12:00 P.M.	Work on TV show
12:00 P.M.– 1:00 P.M.	Lunch
1:00 P.M.– 5:00 P.M.	Work with teacher

The column on the left shows the times when Sara does things. The column on the right tells what Sara does at each time. Put your finger on the times *7:00–8:00,* then move it across to the right. You can see that between 7:00 and 8:00, Sara puts on her makeup.

1. At what time does Sara start working on the TV show?
2. Is this before or after lunch?

Sara starts working at 8:00. You can tell this is before lunch because lunch doesn't start until 12:00. Now answer the following:

3. At what time does Sara start working with her teacher?
4. Is this before or after her TV work?

As you read "A Life on Ice," see what the schedules tell you about David Lee's life.

A Life on Ice

by Shirley Lee

David Lee has his own act in a world-famous ice-skating show. But his act has more to do with fire than with ice.

It's showtime! Groups of skaters, colored lights shining on their costumes, glide through their numbers. The stars delight the watching crowd with jumps, lifts, and spins. Music fills the air.

Then, in the middle of all the skating acts, young David Lee skates into the spotlight. David thrills the crowd with a different kind of act. David juggles while he skates.

Almost faster than the eye can see, David makes rings, hoops, scarves, and clubs seem to dance in the air. Then, David juggles beach balls and spins rings at the same time. He tops all of this when he juggles three flaming torches.

To be in such a large show might seem impossible for one so young. However, David is young only in years. He has been a juggler with the ice show since he was just three years old.

David spends nine months of each year traveling with the ice show. David's life is exciting. But, he must work hard for such a career.

He rises at 8:00 A.M. Then he spends about two hours on schoolwork with his teacher. After his studying is finished, David practices on a banjo for an hour. Then he has a break for lunch.

David's Morning

Time	Activity
8:00 A.M.— 9:00 A.M.	Rise, breakfast
9:00 A.M.—11:00 A.M.	Schoolwork
11:00 A.M.—12:00 P.M.	Banjo practice
12:00 P.M.— 1:00 P.M.	Lunch

After lunch David works on his juggling and skating. Later in the day he may swim, play tennis, or go sightseeing with his parents.

Sometimes David has two or three shows a day. At other times, he has only one show in the evening. No matter what the schedule, David arrives for his act about fifteen minutes ahead of time to warm up. A juggler's hands must be quick and able to move easily. Chilly ice rinks work against this. If a building is really cold, David may wear gloves when he is getting ready.

David changes his act from time to time. "We're always adding new tricks," he says. "My favorite thing is juggling the clubs."

Asked about the dangerous-looking number he does with the flaming torches, David says, "I've been doing the torches since I was seven. I've never been burned. If I catch one wrong, I have several seconds to throw it again before it can burn me."

Everyone who sees the act knows that it is dangerous to juggle torches. David practiced for years before he used them. An amateur juggler should *never* try to do it.

When David drops something—and he doesn't often—he is never flustered. He just picks up the loose object and goes on with his act.

But once the object he dropped was himself. "The week before, we'd had a wide rink," he explains. "The next week it was a narrow one. I was skating backwards and juggling. All of a sudden I went right over the row of lights at the edge of the ice and down on my back."

What did he do? He got right up and started over.

David's contract with the ice show is for one year at a time. Each year, David's father asks him to decide if he wants to sign up for another year. So far David has always decided to keep on with his life on ice.

Checking Comprehension and Skills

1. What kind of an act does David Lee do? (336)
2. What is the most dangerous number that David does? Why is it dangerous? (339)
3. Who decides whether or not David will sign a new contract each year? Why? (340)
4. Would you like to be in a show like David's? Why or why not?

Look at the schedule below in order to answer the first two questions that follow it.

David's Afternoon and Evening

Time	Activity
1:00 P.M.— 3:00 P.M.	Practice juggling and skating
3:00 P.M.— 6:00 P.M.	Free time
6:00 P.M.— 7:00 P.M.	Dinner
7:00 P.M.—10:00 P.M.	Show

•5. At what time does David have a show?
•6. Does David practice before or after dinner?
o7. From what two words is the word we're made?
o8. What two root words are in sightseeing?

•Graphic Aids: Schedules
oStructure: Contractions and Compounds

Reading
Bonus

A Chair for My Mother

by Vera B. Williams

My mother works as a waitress in the Blue Tile Diner. After school sometimes I go to meet her there. Then her boss, Josephine, gives me a job too.

I wash the salts and peppers and fill the ketchups. When I finish, Josephine says, "Good work, honey," and pays me. And every time, I put half of my money into the jar.

It takes a long time to fill a jar this big. Every day when my mother comes home from work, I take down the jar. My mama empties all her change from tips out of her purse for me to count. Then we put all of the coins into the jar.

Sometimes my mama is laughing when she comes home from work. Sometimes she's so tired she falls asleep while I count the money out into piles. Some days she has lots of tips. Some days she has only a little. Then she looks worried. But each evening every single shiny coin goes into the jar.

We sit in the kitchen to count the tips. Usually Grandma sits with us too. While we count, she likes to hum. Often she has money in her old leather wallet for us. Whenever she gets a good bargain on something she buys, she puts the savings into the jar.

When we can't get a single other coin into the jar, we are going to take out all the money. Then we will go and buy a chair.

Yes, a chair. A wonderful, beautiful, fat, soft armchair. We'll get one covered in velvet with roses all over it. We're going to get the best chair in the whole world.

That is because our old chairs burned up. There was a big fire in our other house. All our chairs burned. So did our sofa and so did everything else. That wasn't such a long time ago.

My mother and I were walking to our house from the bus. We were looking at everyone's tulips. Then we came to our block.

Right outside our house stood two big fire engines. I could see lots of smoke. Tall orange flames came out of the roof. All the neighbors stood in a bunch across the street. Mama grabbed my hand and we ran. My uncle Sandy saw us and ran to us. Mama yelled, "Where's Mother?" I yelled, "Where's my grandma?" Aunt Ida waved and shouted, "She's here. She's OK. Don't worry."

Grandma was all right. Our cat was safe too, though it took a while to find her. But everything else in our house was spoiled.

What was left of the house was only ashes.

We went to stay with Aunt Ida and Uncle Sandy. Then, later, we were able to move into the apartment downstairs. We painted the walls yellow. The floors were all shiny. But the rooms were very empty.

The first day we moved in the neighbors brought lots of food. And they brought other things too. The family across the street brought a table and three kitchen chairs. The very old man next door gave us a bed from when his children were little.

My other grandpa brought us his beautiful rug. Aunt Sally made us some red-and-white curtains. Mama's boss, Josephine, brought pots and pans, silverware, and dishes.

Everyone clapped when my grandma made a speech. "You are all the kindest people," she said, "and we thank you very much. It's lucky we're young and can start all over."

That was last year, but we still have no sofa and no big chairs. When Mama comes home, her feet hurt. "There's no good place for me to take a load off my feet," she says. When Grandma wants to cut up potatoes, she has to sit on a hard kitchen chair.

So that is why Mama brought home the biggest jar she could find at the diner. And that is why all the coins started to go into the jar.

After supper one night this week, Mama and Grandma and I stood in front of the jar. "Well, I never would have believed it, but I guess it's full," Mama said.

My mother brought home little paper wrappers for the nickels and the dimes and the quarters. I counted them all out and wrapped them all up.

On my mother's day off, we took all the coins to the bank. The bank exchanged them for ten-dollar bills. Then we took the bus downtown to shop for our chair.

We shopped through four furniture stores. We tried out big and small chairs, high and low chairs, soft chairs and harder ones. Grandma said she felt like Goldilocks in "The Three Bears" trying out all the chairs.

Finally we found the chair we were all dreaming of. And the money from the jar was enough to pay for it. We called Aunt Ida and Uncle Sandy. They came right down in their pickup truck to drive the chair home for us. They knew we couldn't wait for it to be delivered.

We set the chair right beside the window with the red-and-white curtains. Grandma and Mama and I all sat in it while Aunt Ida took our picture.

Now Grandma sits in it and talks with people going by in the daytime. Mama sits down and watches the news on TV when she comes home from her job. After supper, I sit with her. And she can reach right up and turn out the light if I fall asleep in her lap.

Reading More Than Just Words

Have you ever tried to learn how to do a hard trick? Maybe you wanted to know how to skate in a figure eight or how to juggle three oranges. So you found a book about the trick. Chances are that you could not learn to do your trick just by reading the words in the book. You had to look at the pictures too.

Sharpen Your Skills

When you read, you sometimes need more than just words to understand an idea. Words can work together with other kinds of information, such as maps, graphs, or schedules. You need to look at these things too.

The article on the next two pages has a schedule and a graph. Use them, as well as the words, to help you find out about people's first trips to the moon.

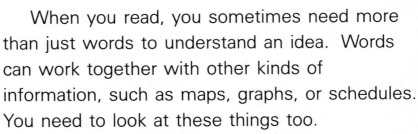

People on the Moon

People first went from Earth to the moon and back in 1969. Three Americans flew in the *Apollo 11* spacecraft. Their trip took eight days in all. This was not long when you think that they flew over 244,000[1] miles each way.

When *Apollo 11* reached the moon, it separated into two parts. One astronaut stayed in the command ship. This ship kept going around and around the moon. Two other men landed on the moon in the *Eagle,* the landing craft. The schedule below shows the main events of the *Apollo 11* trip.

---

1. about 394,000 kilometers

Apollo 11 Schedule

Day	Time	Event
July 16	9:32 A.M.	Blastoff from Cape Kennedy, Florida
July 19	1:22 P.M.	*Apollo 11* goes into orbit around moon
July 20	4:17 P.M.	*Eagle* lands on the moon
July 20	10:56 P.M.	First person steps onto the moon
July 24	12:40 P.M.	*Apollo 11* splashes down in Pacific Ocean on Earth

After spending about 21 hours on the moon, the *Eagle* flew back to the command ship. Then *Apollo 11* went back to Earth.

Since 1969, other ships have traveled from Earth to the moon. People have stayed on the moon longer than 21 hours. The graph on this page shows how long some of the crews have stayed on the moon.

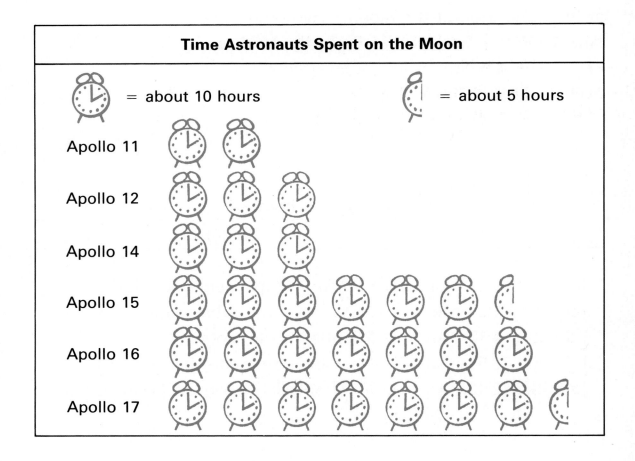

Time Astronauts Spent on the Moon

= about 10 hours   = about 5 hours

Apollo 11

Apollo 12

Apollo 14

Apollo 15

Apollo 16

Apollo 17

To get all the facts from pages 351 and 352, you need to study the words, the schedule, and the graph.

By reading only the paragraphs on pages 351 and 352, you could learn that people have gone to the moon. You could get an idea of what happened on the *Apollo 11* trip. You could also learn that other crews have stayed longer on the moon than the *Apollo 11* crew.

If you wanted more details about *Apollo 11,* you would turn to the schedule on page 351. There you could find out when the main events of that trip happened.

If you wanted to compare the *Apollo 11* trip to later trips to the moon, you would use the graph on page 352. It quickly shows how much longer other crews stayed on the moon.

1. When did the first person step onto the moon? Where did you find this fact?
2. Which *Apollo* crew spent the most time on the moon? Where did you find this fact?

Check some of your other schoolbooks to see how words work together with schedules, graphs, or maps to explain ideas.

Books to Read

The Day of Ahmed's Secret
by Florence Parry Heide
and Judith Heide Gilliland

Ahmed carries fuel in his donkey cart all over Cairo, a large city in Egypt. As Ahmed goes about his work, he keeps thinking of nightfall when he can share a secret with his family.

Mom Can't See Me by Sally Hobart Alexander

"Mostly she's like other mothers," Leslie Alexander says of her mother. For example, Leslie explains, her mother camps out, swims, rides a bike, and laughs a lot. Leading a rich, full life seems easy for Leslie's mother. You'd never guess she has been blind for many years.

Twenty Ways to Lose Your Best Friend
by Marilyn Singer

When tryouts are held for the class play, Emma has a choice. She can vote for her friend Sandy, who is a terrible actress, or she can vote for stuck-up Marguerite. Emma votes for Marguerite. Will she lose her best friend?

Section Ten
Take a Closer Look

What Does It Look Like to You?

When you look at a cloud, you can often imagine that it looks like something else, such as an animal. But clouds move so fast that they are always changing. One moment a cloud may look like a rabbit. Then, a moment later, it may look more like a bear.

You can also imagine that a mountain, an island, a tree, or another place in nature looks like something else. People like to name such places.

The photograph shows a mountainside in New Hampshire. It is called The Old Man of the Mountain. Can you see why it is called that?

The Sleeping Birds

The heat of the sun bounced off the rocky hills ahead. The hot air seemed to dance in waves over the sandy desert. As Tina and Linda walked toward the hills, they could even feel the warmth through their shoes. The two girls enjoyed the brightness of the spring desert flowers. They laughed at the quickness of a desert mouse. They carefully felt the sharpness of a cactus.

Linda was visiting her cousin, Tina, who lived in the desert. Linda lived in the city. Now Linda said, "I always knew the desert was dry. But I didn't know it could be so beautiful."

"The desert is dry," Tina agreed, "and it can be beautiful. It also has all kinds of interesting things. Just wait until you see my special place."

Soon the sun began to set behind a high, rocky hill. The warm desert breeze had the softness of a feather.

Tina stopped and looked pleased. "Here is the special place I wanted to show you. It's called 'Two Sleeping Birds.'"

"This is a lovely place," said Linda. "But where are the sleeping birds?"

"Look where the sun is setting," said Tina as she pointed. "See that big rock with the little rocks on top. Now can you see the two sleeping birds?"

"Yes. It was worth the walk out here," Linda laughed, "and *back!*"

Sharpen Your Skills

Details in a story or an article can help you picture what is happening.
1. What details helped you picture the desert?
2. What details helped you picture Tina's special place?

As you read "Grizzly Bears' Lodge," the details can help you picture what is happening.

Grizzly Bears' Lodge

retold by Sue Alexander

*In the northeast corner of the state of
Wyoming, a huge tower of solid rock stands high
above the surrounding land. Today this rocky
tower is called* The Devil's Tower. *Long ago the
Sioux Indians called it* Grizzly Bears' Lodge.
This is the story they told about it.

Long ago, near the place where the tower
now stands, there was a Sioux village. One
day three young girls left the village and went
out to play on the prairie.

It was early summer. The girls smelled the
sweetness of the new grass. They saw that
some wildflowers were blooming. The flowers
covered the earth like a yellow and white and
pink and blue carpet. The girls picked so
many flowers that soon their arms were full.

But just as the girls started home, they heard a terrible roar. Suddenly three huge and hairy grizzly bears with sharp, shiny teeth appeared. The bears began to chase the three girls.

In those days the land in that place was almost flat. There was just one small rock, standing a few feet high. The young girls ran to this rock and climbed up on top of it.

But looking back, the girls could see that the bears were coming. And soon the three bears would climb the rock too.

"Help! Help!" cried the first girl.

"Please save us!" cried the second girl.

"Oh, please! Won't somebody help us!" cried the third girl.

Then, just as the bears got near the rock, the rock began to grow higher. Just as the bears jumped at the rock, the rock grew even higher. Just as the bears tried to climb the rock, the rock grew higher still.

The girls kept calling, the bears kept climbing, and the rock kept growing. Higher and higher, it grew.

As the rock grew higher, the three girls kept calling for help. As the bears climbed up the rock, their claws dug deep grooves into it.

At last the rock was so high and its sides were so steep and slippery that the three bears fell all the way down. They fell to the ground below and were still.

For a long time the girls watched from the top of the rock. Finally, the stillness below convinced them that the bears must be dead. So they decided it was safe to go down.

But how could they get down?

The rock was now far too high to jump down and far too steep and slippery to climb down.

Then they had an idea.

The three girls braided the flowers they had picked into a long rope. One by one the girls climbed down the rope of flowers to the ground. Then, as fast as they could, they hurried back to the safety of their village.

All this happened long, long ago. But, if you visit Grizzly Bears' Lodge *today, you can still see the long, deep grooves made by the bears on the sides of the huge rock.*

Checking Comprehension and Skills

•1. What details in the story helped you picture and hear the three grizzly bears that chased the Sioux girls? (361)

2. How do you think the girls felt when they saw the bears coming up to the rock they had climbed on? How do you think they felt after the rock began to grow?

•3. What details helped you picture the rock as it grew? (363)

4. When the bears were dead, what did the girls want to do? How did they get what they wanted? (363-364)

5. How could you tell that the "Grizzly Bears' Lodge" is fiction?

6. Take another look at the picture on page 356. Make up a short story to explain how the mountain came to look like a person.

Which word would you use in this sentence?
o7. The ____ of the house told us no one was there.
greatness   stillness   gentleness

• Details
o Structure: Suffixes (-y, -ness)

Now You See It—
Now You Don't!

Look at these pictures. Can you see an insect, an owl, a toad, a deer, and a hare? They all blend into their backgrounds. This is because they all have natural camouflage.

What is camouflage? It is anything that can keep an animal from being seen easily. It can be an animal's color or shape.

What good is camouflage? Some animals are always being hunted by other animals. By being hard to see, they can often escape. Other animals are always hunting. By being hard to see, they can get closer to their victims before they are seen.

Figuring Out the Main Idea

What kind of animal do all the photos on this page show? Yes, fish. Are these fish difficult or easy to see? In a sentence, you might say, "These fish are hard to see."

Sharpen Your Skills

The last sentence above gives the most important idea from the pictures. When you read, you need to find the most important idea in a paragraph, the **main idea.** This idea isn't always told in any one sentence. Here is how to figure out the main idea when it is not stated:

1. Find the topic. The **topic** is what a paragraph is mostly about. Usually you can say what the topic is in a word or two.
2. Think about all the information in the paragraph and figure out the most important idea about the topic—the main idea.

3. Look for **details,** small pieces of information that tell more about the main idea.

Figure out the main idea of this paragraph:

Some fish hide from enemies by changing color to match the bottom of the sea. Others have a fake eye in their tails, so enemies attack the wrong end! Some fish are difficult to spot because they are as blue as the water.

1. What is the topic of the paragraph?
2. Which sentence tells the main idea?
   a. Some fish have the wrong end in front.
   b. Fish have different ways to fool enemies.
3. What details tell more about the main idea?

The topic is fish. The main idea is *b.* Fish that change color, fish that have fake eyes, and fish that are the color of water are details.
Now read the last paragraph on page 367 again.

4. What is the topic of the paragraph?
5. Which sentence tells the main idea?
   a. Camouflage helps animals survive.
   b. It's hard for small animals to escape.
6. What details tell more about the main idea?

Look for main ideas in the next article.

Animals in the Far North

by Karen Herzoff

The Far North

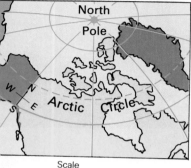

North Pole

Arctic Circle

Scale

0 400 800 1200 miles

0   800   1600 kilometers

KEY

■ Alaska (U.S.)

□ Canada

■ Greenland

Arctic, the far north part of the earth (see the map)

camouflage, shape or coloring of an animal that hides it

When you think of the Arctic and the far north, what words come to your mind? Cold? Snow? Ice? How do animals that live there survive? How do they find food? How do some animals hide so they do not become food?

The **Arctic** and the far north are very cold, and there is lots of snow and ice for most of the year. Animals that live in the far north are protected in the same way as some animals in other parts of the world—by **camouflage.** They are about the same color as their background. This makes them hard to see. Bigger animals looking for food cannot find them easily.

A ptarmigan in the winter

The Hunted

For several months each year, the far north has "summer." Flowers bloom, vegetables grow, and food is plentiful. In summer the trees and grass are brown and gray. The animals are brown and gray to match the colors of summer.

In winter, the far north is white with snow. Some animals turn white too. The arctic hare turns snowy white. However, the tips of its ears stay black all year. They look like misfits above its white coat. The arctic lemming, a very small animal, also turns white in winter. One kind of bird, the ptarmigan, changes too. The ptarmigan's feathers are white in the winter and brown in the summer.

Have You Heard?

Arctic animals that change color really just get new fur or feathers. The fur or feathers of one color drop out as new fur or feathers of the other color grow.

A ptarmigan in the summer

This arctic hare looks misplaced. It is white, but no snow has fallen yet.

Sometimes, however, these small animals and birds do not match their backgrounds. Snow may come early in the fall. Then many animals are still brown when the ground is already white. Or snow may come late in the spring. The animals have turned brown and gray by then, but the ground is white. The animals look like they are misplaced. The animals must protect themselves in other ways until their coloring agrees with the weather.

The Hunters

Some arctic animals that hunt change color too, but not for safety. They need to hide when they hunt. Then they can sneak up on other animals and catch them for food. The arctic fox is a hunter. The fox is brown in summer. Its brown fur becomes white in winter. Weasels are brown in summer and white in winter too. One spot of black stays at the tips of their tails all year round.

A weasel has caught a mouse.

Some northern animals that hunt stay white all year. They live so far north that there is always snow on the ground. The arctic wolf is an animal that has a light yellowish-white coat all year. The polar bear is another hunter whose coat remains white all year. Many seals have had the misfortune to mistake this large, white bear for a pile of snow.

Mother and cub
polar bears

An arctic wolf

A Lion Is Hungry!

by D. S. Stock

As the sun begins to set on a grassland in Africa, a lion wakes up from a long nap. The lion is hungry and goes off to look for food. Walking through some tall, waving grasses, the lion is hidden. The grasses are all different colors—brown, gold, green, and red.

Up ahead the lion sees a few trees, some bushes, and more tall grass. The lion cannot see the black-and-cream stripes of the zebras standing quietly in the distance. Lions are color-blind. They see everything in shades of gray—the zebras, the grasses, and even the trees. Since the zebra herd is not moving, it blends into the background. If it were moving, the lion would see it.

Not seeing anything, the lion goes off in another direction in its search for food. Soon the lion is following a herd of antelopes. The lion is waiting for one of the antelopes to fall behind the rest. The lion stays in the tall grasses as a precaution against being seen.

Now the sun has gone down. The lion is still following the herd. Suddenly, the lion sees a small antelope fall behind. But the lion meets misfortune as it sneaks up. The antelopes are wide-awake and very swift. In one second the whole herd takes off. The small antelope that the lion was watching runs off with the others.

The lion is still hungry. It will have to keep on searching until it finds food.

Checking Comprehension and Skills

1. What is camouflage? (370)
2. What color would an animal be if it were camouflaged and lived where there was snow? If the animal were camouflaged and lived where there was a lot of green grass or leaves, what color would it probably be?
•3. Read paragraph two on page 374. Which of the sentences below states the main idea of the paragraph? Which sentence states a detail of the paragraph?

   a. Camouflage protects the zebras from the lion.

   b. The zebra herd is not moving.
4. If you could be an animal protected by camouflage, what animal would you be? What would your shape or coloring be?
5. What did you learn from this selection that you didn't know before?

Which word would you use in this sentence?
○6. She wore a raincoat as a ____ against rain.

   precaution   prairie   problem

• Main idea and supporting details
○ Structure: Prefixes (pre-, mis-)

Easy-to-Fix Trail Mix

To see the beauty in nature, you can go out for a hike. Hiking makes a person hungry! Before you go, make this tasty snack to carry along.

1. Get: $\frac{1}{2}$ cup of roasted split soybeans
   $\frac{1}{2}$ cup of carob bits
   1 cup of raisins
   1 cup of raw sunflower seeds
   1 cup of peanuts

2. Mix them together well.

3. Put your trail mix in a plastic bag to keep it dry and fresh.

4. Enjoy the trail mix on your hike! You will even have enough to share with a friend!

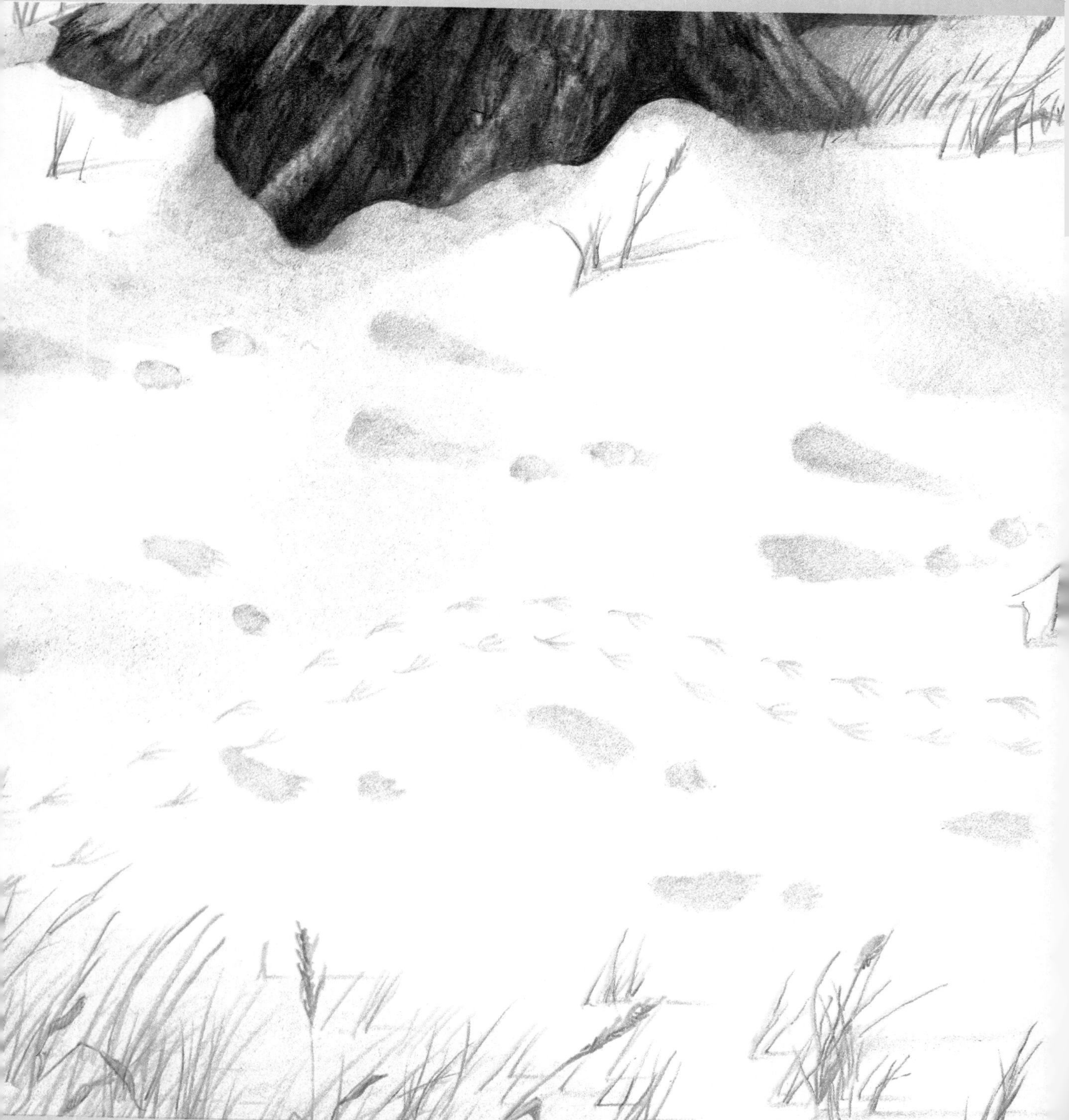

Whose Tracks Are These?

by David McCord

So you found some fresh tracks in the snow?
And what made them? You say you don't know?
    Were they two pairs of skis?
    Rabbits down on their knees?
Or a skunk with a splint on his toe?

Follow the Signs

Animals often leave signs that show where they have been. The signs can be tracks or nests or bits of fur or feathers. If you look, you may find signs of animals all around you.

In the city you can find clues that show where an animal has been. Be on the lookout. A feather or an empty nest is a sign of birds. A hole in the ground may show where a squirrel buried some food.

In the country you can find many animal signs. Holes in a tree trunk show where a woodpecker was eating. A discarded snake skin tells you that a snake grew larger and shed its old skin. Tooth marks on a fallen tree alert you to watch for a beaver dam.

When you learn how to read and follow animal signs, you can discover many things from them. Often you can find out what kind of animal was passing by and something about its life.

Sharpen Your Skills

The **topic** of an article is a word or two that tells what the whole article is about. The **main idea** is the most important idea about the topic. **Supporting details** tell something about the main idea.

1. In a word or two, what is the topic of this article?
2. What is the main idea of this article?
   a. Feathers and empty nests show you that birds have been in a place.
   b. You can find animal signs all around you.
3. What details tell you where to look for animal signs?

When you read the next two articles, try to figure out the main idea of each one.

Animals at Home

by Theresa Reinhard

When you go for a walk or a hike, you may not see any wild animals. Does this mean there are none? No. Most places where you can walk are filled with animal life. Different kinds of animals live everywhere— above ground, below ground, and under water. But animals that are afraid of people will stay hidden while you walk nearby. You can tell which animals live there by being on the lookout for their homes. If you know what to look for, you can see telltale signs of animal homes everywhere.

Above Ground

Don't always look down to find signs of wildlife. Look up too. As you walk you may see signs of animal homes that were built above ground. If you notice a nest of leaves, moss, and grass that is rounded in shape, it is a squirrel's home. Squirrels' nests are usually larger than birds' nests.

A robin's nest

A squirrel's nest

Below Ground

In the open places of the western plains, look for signs of prairie dogs. These burrowing animals live in large "towns." A prairie dog digs about twelve feet[1] straight down. After digging many tunnels, it digs upward to make a back door.

How can you find a prairie dog's burrow if it is twelve feet below the earth? You will be able to find it by locating the dirt the small animal piles around each door.

---

1. about $3\frac{1}{2}$ meters

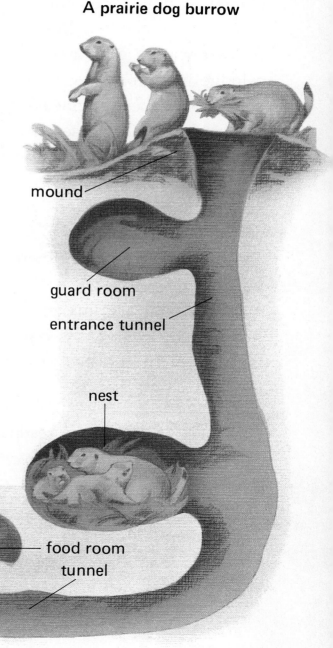

A prairie dog burrow

mound

guard room

entrance tunnel

nest

food room

tunnel

In the Water

Whenever you see a stream or pond, look for signs of animals that live in or near water. You may see a lodge made by beavers— some of the best engineers in the world! You will see that the lodge is never far from shore. The part that rises above the water is a pile of sticks and twigs. It is shaped like an upside-down bowl.

A muskrat also makes its home in the water. Its home is different from a beaver's in at least two ways. First, it is smaller. Second, it is made of plants and reeds, not sticks and trees.

Next time you take a walk, remember to look for some animal homes. Don't let the animals fool you into thinking they are not around. Their watchfulness is protecting them from uninvited visitors. But now that you know where to look for some of their homes, you may even see where they are hiding.

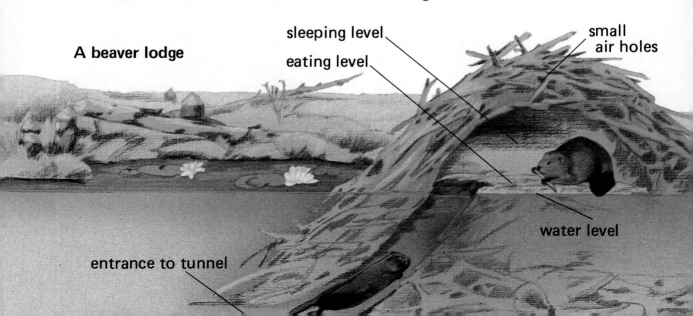

A beaver lodge

sleeping level

eating level

small air holes

water level

entrance to tunnel

Fossil Hunt
in the City

by Merrill and Jennifer Horenstein
as told to Sallie Luther

I couldn't believe what my sister, Merrill, had just told me. "Fossils in the middle of Manhattan?" I asked her again.

"Yes, Jenny," she said. "Manhattan is full of them."

We were walking down New York City's Fifth Avenue. Merrill's hobby is finding fossils. Now she was taking me on my first "hunt," right here in Manhattan.

But instead of picks and shovels, our tools were books and magnifying glasses. The fossils we were hunting were "buried" in the walls of buildings.

"How did they get in buildings?" I asked.

"Well," Merrill explained, "many, many years ago, some oceans dried up and turned into rock—first limestone, then marble. When the oceans dried up, the rock was left behind, with fossils trapped in it.

"Today people cut big blocks of marble and limestone from giant pits," she went on. "They use those blocks to build buildings. But come on—there is lots to see!"

As we walked along, Merrill pointed out the fossils in many of the buildings we passed. She had learned about them from our father. He is a scientist who studies fossils. He works at a museum here in New York City.

There were fossils everywhere. At a big department store, we saw some in a light yellow wall. At a bank, we spotted giant ones in a wall in the lobby.

It was also fun to watch people watch *us*. At one building, Merrill started to show me a rosy-red wall of marble from France. A guard asked us uneasily what we were doing. When we told him we were on a fossil hunt, he looked at us as if we were crazy. Then

Merrill handed him her magnifying glass so he could look too.

"Well, what do you know!" the man exclaimed. "I've been here for years, and I've never even noticed those things. Thanks!"

As we left, he was still looking at the wall. It made me want to tell everyone about the treasures all around them.

By the time we got to another large store, I was beginning to think I could spot fossils anywhere.

"OK, Jenny," Merrill said. "Point them out to me." But no matter how hard I looked, I couldn't see a single one. Then she pointed at the tall columns at different places on the floor. And there they were in some smooth, brown limestone from Missouri. Each looked like the spokes of a tiny wheel.

We finished up our hunt at Dad's office in the museum. He took us to see *his* favorite fossils. The neatest one was a big snail from Germany. It was beneath a wall vent on the first floor—almost under people's feet.

We talked about our "hunt" all the way home. Boy, it was going to be great visiting other cities. Now any building made out of marble or limestone could be a place for a fossil hunt. You never know what you might find!

Checking Comprehension and Skills

•1. Which of the following is the topic, the main idea, and a detail of "Animals at Home"?
   a. Squirrels' nests are bigger than birds' nests.
   b. Animals live in many different places.
   c. wildlife

 2. What were Merrill and Jenny looking for in Manhattan? (385)

•3. Read the lines below. Which is the topic, the main idea, and a detail of "Fossil Hunt in the City"?
   a. fossils
   b. The girls used magnifying glasses.
   c. Fossils can be found in city buildings.

 4. Why is Merrill's hobby unusual?

 5. Tell about the most unusual hobby you have heard or read about.

   Which word would you use in this sentence?
○6. Dad asked us ＿＿ why we were painting the chair.
   unless   understand   uneasily

• Main idea and supporting details
○ Structure: Prefixes, Suffixes, and Endings

What Makes Sense?

James is listening to <u>rock</u> music.

Which picture do you think goes with the sentence above? Both pictures show a meaning for the word *rock*, but picture *A* makes better sense than picture *B*.

Like *rock*, many words have more than one meaning. If you're confused by something you read, maybe a word has a meaning other than the one you know about. If this happens, stop. Read again the part that confused you. Ask, "What meaning would make sense here?" Try to figure out one that makes sense. Then check yourself. Look up any word you aren't sure of in a dictionary or a glossary.

Remember, words can have more than one meaning. Choose the one that makes sense!

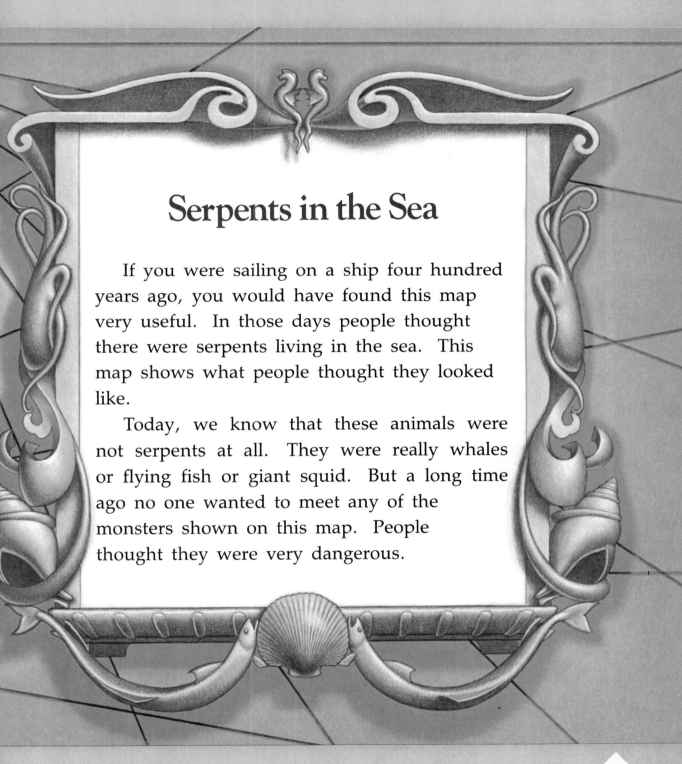

Serpents in the Sea

If you were sailing on a ship four hundred years ago, you would have found this map very useful. In those days people thought there were serpents living in the sea. This map shows what people thought they looked like.

Today, we know that these animals were not serpents at all. They were really whales or flying fish or giant squid. But a long time ago no one wanted to meet any of the monsters shown on this map. People thought they were very dangerous.

What Is Out There?

"Watch out, miss!" a voice yelled down to Susan. She had been standing on the deck of the *Primrose*, a large sailing ship, staring into the water.

A barrel tumbled off the deck above her. Susan pulled her long skirt out of the way just as it rolled past her.

"Are you all right, miss?" a sailor named Bill asked her.

"I'm fine. I thought I saw something in the water." She took off her bonnet and looked again.

"I don't see anything," Bill said. "But there are strange things in the sea. Once, I saw an animal as big as this ship swimming along next to us."

"A serpent?" Susan's eyes lit up.

"I thought so," Bill said. "Another time I saw a fish that flew through the air."

Susan smiled as she thought about a fish flying through the air.

"I'd really like to see one," she said.

"I'd rather see a fish that flies than a giant animal with eight arms," Bill said.

"Eight!" Susan said excitedly.

"Well, I think it had eight. We sailed away from it so quickly that I didn't have time to count them carefully. You keep your eyes open, miss. You're sure to see something unusual in these waters."

Sharpen Your Skills

As you read, you often have to figure things out on your own. You can do this by thinking about the details in the story.

1. What details in the story tell you that it took place long ago?
2. Was Susan excited by Bill's stories of sea animals? What details tell you that?

Look for details in the next story that help you understand the special kind of serpent Cyrus is.

Cyrus, the Unsinkable Sea Serpent

by Bill Peet

Once upon a time there was a giant sea serpent named Cyrus. Even though he was an ugly-looking monster he wasn't the least bit mean. All he ever did was swim in the sea. He had no idea of where he was going.

One day Cyrus said, "I wish there was something more exciting to do. I'd like to have some fun for a change."

He swam along until he came to a harbor. A ship was about to set sail. From all the talking, Cyrus learned that the ship was the *Primrose*.

It was headed for a new land. The passengers were poor people who were going there to find a better life.

As the ship moved away from the dock, the loud voice of an old man called out. "A storm will take you under! If a storm doesn't get you, the pirates will! You'll never make it, I say!"

Cyrus was worried about the *Primrose*'s passengers. He dived under the water and came up half a mile behind the ship. Cyrus didn't want to scare anyone. So he was careful to keep out of sight.

For three days the ship sailed along without the least bit of trouble. Then on the fourth day just before the sun set, black clouds came rolling over the horizon. There was a rumble of thunder. The wind blew hard.

"Everyone below!" ordered the captain.

Just as the passengers went below, a giant wave crashed over the bow of the ship. More waves followed— great, towering waves.

Cyrus saw that the ship could not last out the storm. He reached the *Primrose* just as it was about to go down.

He threw himself around the ship. Then, gulping in air, he puffed himself up into a giant life preserver. Now Cyrus was unsinkable. With a tight hold on the ship he carried it high over the waves.

He held the *Primrose* up this way until the storm was over. Shouts of joy came from the people on the ship. "I thought we would sink!" cried the captain.

"So did I," sighed Cyrus as he watched the ship sail away. He was much too tired to go on. He flopped down on the sea to sleep.

When the sea serpent woke up, the *Primrose* was gone. Cyrus searched the sea for miles and miles. He was about to give up when he sighted a ship on the horizon.

As Cyrus came closer he saw that *this* ship was flying a black flag. It was a pirate ship! On ahead he saw the *Primrose*.

Then to Cyrus's surprise the pirates opened fire. Twenty cannons blasted the masts of the *Primrose* to pieces.

"I'll fix those pirates," snarled Cyrus.

Quickly he dived deep into the sea. Then he shot straight up at the pirate ship.

Cyrus's hard head hit the ship right in the center—KER-WHAM!!! The ship cracked into pieces.

The pirate ship was wrecked and so was Cyrus. He had knocked himself out. His eyes were spinning like pinwheels. He sank below the waves as limp as an old shoestring.

When he finally came up, he was surprised to find only bits of the pirate ship left. The pirates, wondering what had hit them, had hopped aboard a piece of the ship.

The passengers of the *Primrose* had seen the giant sea monster wreck the pirate ship. They were afraid their ship would be next.

"We're done for," said
the captain. "That old man
was right. He said the trip
would end in trouble.
Remember?"

"Who could forget him?"
Cyrus said to himself. "The
old man was right about the
storm and the pirates. But
he didn't know about me."

Cyrus had slipped quietly
up to the front of the ship.
He looked at the anchor
chain. Then he put the
chain tightly between his
teeth. He pulled it until the
ship moved, bringing cries of
fear from the people.

"It's the sea monster!
He's carrying us off to his
cave! He'll eat us alive!"

"Hold it!" roared the
captain. "Maybe he means
to help. After all, he
wrecked the pirate ship.
And look! He's taking us
west! If he keeps going,
we'll hit land. So let's all
cool down and enjoy the
ride!"

Like a high-stepping horse, Cyrus galloped over the sea. Never had a sailing ship moved so fast. Cyrus kept the *Primrose* moving night and day.

Finally one morning a sailor shouted, "Land ho! Land ho!" Sure enough, land appeared over the horizon.

At last the dangerous trip was over. With one last burst of speed Cyrus carried the *Primrose* up on the beach. Then he headed out to sea. As he swam away, everyone gave him a loud cheer.

"This has been exciting enough to last a while," Cyrus said. "Now what I need is a good long rest."

He swam until he found a little island. He settled down in the trees and slept for a whole month. Cyrus was very tired for some reason or other.

Checking Comprehension and Skills

1. Who was Cyrus? (396)
2. Why did he follow the *Primrose?* (397)
•3. Page 396 says that Cyrus was not mean. Do you agree? Why do you think as you do?
4. How do you think Cyrus felt when the pirates fired at the *Primrose?*
•5. Why was Cyrus very tired at the end of the story?
6. Do you think Cyrus will want to follow another ship again? Why do you think as you do?
7. Cyrus was able to help the *Primrose* because he was very large in size. How might he have helped the ship if he had been small?

Which word would you use in each sentence?
○8. The ship fired its ____ at the pirates.
   canvas   cannot   cannons
○9. He ____ down in the big chair.
   selling   settled   shelter

• Drawing conclusions
○ Structure: Syllables

Dragons

Today, no one talks about seeing dragons. But many years ago, everybody believed in them.

People believed that dragons stole money and treasure, killed crops and people, and spread sickness. In stories, very brave people fought dragons. Most people just tried to stay away from them.

No one believes in dragons now. Do you think people can be wrong?

Seeing Likenesses and Differences

How are all of the animals in the pictures alike? They are all lizards. What are some differences you notice? Do any of the lizards remind you of the dragon shown on page 404?

Sharpen Your Skills

You were able to point out likenesses and differences in the pictures. When you read, you also need to understand how things are alike or different. Sometimes an author uses clue words that help you do this. The words in the box are a few of the words that can help you see how things are alike and how they are different.

same	like	however	not	unlike

On page 407, read to find out how a "flying dragon" is like the dragons in stories.

The flying dragon glides through the air from tree to tree. With its thin wings spread, it looks something like a dragon in a story. It even has the same name. However, the flying dragon is a lizard. It's much smaller than a story dragon—only about eight inches[1] long. Unlike a story dragon, it eats ants, not people.

1. In what two ways is this lizard like a dragon in a story?
2. What clue words helped you answer number 1?

Did you say that its wings make the lizard look like a dragon and that its name is the same? The clue words *like* and *same* should have helped you. Now go back to find out how the flying dragon is different from a story dragon.

3. In what two ways is this lizard different from a dragon in a story?
4. What clue words helped you answer number 3?

See what is alike and what is different in the next two articles.

---

1. 20 centimeters

The Dragons of Komodo

by

Tom Wolczak

Have you ever seen pictures of dragons in books of stories? The dragons have two or four legs. Sometimes they have two wings. Almost always they have a long tail. They live in caves and grow to be very large. Their teeth and claws are very sharp, and they breathe fire.

There are some dragons that don't live in books. They are the Komodo dragons, the largest lizards in the world. They are very much alive on the island of Komodo.

Komodo dragons have legs, tails, teeth, and claws like those of dragons in books. But they don't have wings and they can't fly. They have long, yellow tongues, but they don't breathe fire. They are not as big as dragons in stories, but they do grow to be nine to twelve feet[1] long.

---

1. over $2\frac{1}{2}$ to $3\frac{1}{2}$ meters

A man named P. A. Ouwens brought the Komodo dragons to the world's attention. He worked at a museum on an island near Komodo. In 1912 someone brought him a lizard skin. It was over nine feet[1] long. The person told Ouwens it was from a *small* lizard from the island of Komodo.

Ouwens sent people to Komodo to look for the lizards, and they brought back more skins. Ouwens wrote about the lizards and named them.

In 1926 Douglas and Babs Burden went to Komodo to learn about the lizards. They brought two live Komodo dragons back to the United States. Almost thirty thousand people a day went to see the dragons at a zoo in New York City. And no wonder. Suddenly, animals that were only in books could be seen alive!

1. over $2\frac{1}{2}$ meters

Dragons of the Sea

by Bill Keenan

The animal in this picture has black, scaly skin. It swims in the sea. It looks something like a small dragon. Is it something from a frightening movie? No! It's a strange lizard called the marine iguana.

This kind of lizard is very different from all other lizards. It is the only one in the world that dives into the sea to find food.

Marine iguanas are found only on the Galápagos[1] Islands. Scientists think that, long ago, the ocean brought land iguanas from the west coast of South America. These lizards rode on floating clumps of logs and mud. On the Galápagos, the lizards were able to live best near the sea. They found seaweed on the shore to eat. They learned to swim. They learned to dive to reach plants growing under the water.

---

1. Galápagos (gə lä'pə gəs)

Like many land iguanas, the Galápagos iguanas can grow to be three to five feet[1] long. But, unlike the others, the Galápagos lizards have feet that are partly webbed. Their bodies look like big lumps of black rock along the shore. Enemies such as hawks have a hard time seeing them from the air.

The Galápagos iguanas look fierce. But they are very gentle most of the time. They gather in large, peaceful groups. They lie on the rocks and stay warm in the sun.

Once a day, though, they leave their cozy rocks to go into the water. They don't seem to like swimming in the cool water. They prefer staying on the rocks. But they must search for food. They often dive thirty feet[2] deep. They look for rocks covered with seaweed. When a lizard finds such a rock, it holds on to the rock with its long, curved claws. Then it tears off the plants with its rough teeth.

Generally after five or ten minutes, the lizard comes up for air. Then it dives again. As it does this, it looks almost like a sea monster!

---

1. about 1 to 1½ meters   2. about 9 meters

These large lizards drink their water from the ocean too. Drinking only ocean water would kill most other animals. The salt would get into their blood and poison them. But the marine iguana has certain parts inside its nose. These parts take the extra salt out of the lizard's blood. They store the salt. When these parts get full, the lizard shoots a very salty spray out of its nose. The lizard can also shoot its spray over twelve inches[1] to scare off an enemy. This mean-looking lizard doesn't breathe fire. But you can guess why it might be called a "dragon"!

---

1. 30 centimeters

Checking Comprehension and Skills

1. What are dragons in books of stories supposed to look like? (408)
•2. Why do you think the lizards on Komodo are called "dragons"?
•3. How is the Komodo dragon not like dragons in stories? (408)
•4. Why do some people think the marine iguana is like a dragon?
•5. Both the marine iguana and the Komodo dragon are lizards that look scary. How are they different from each other?
6. Would you rather come face to face with a Komodo dragon or a marine iguana? Why?
7. Why might it be fun to have a Komodo dragon for a pet? What problems might you have?

Which word would you use in each sentence?
○8. Do you ___ swimming or bike riding?
pretend   prefer   power
○9. A blanket feels ___ on a cold night.
cozy   canal   city

• Comparative relationships
○ Structure: Syllables

Monsters of the Movies

Hold your breath! Grab your chair! Scream and shut your eyes! The monsters are on the screen again.

They are bigger than anything on earth. They are meaner and more trouble than anything you have ever seen.

Get a good seat. The show is about to begin!

King Kong

The gorilla in this picture is King Kong. In 1933 he starred in the movie *King Kong*. The movie was about a fierce gorilla taken from Africa and brought to New York City. The movie was a big hit across the nation.

King Kong was supposed to look fifty feet[1] tall. His giant hand looked eight feet[2] long. He could climb tall buildings and crush airplanes with one hand.

Do you think King Kong was a real gorilla? Of course not! A real one grows to be only six feet[3] tall. A gorilla can lift something that is four hundred pounds.[4] That's a strong animal, but certainly not as strong as King Kong.

A real gorilla is usually friendly. It spends most of its day just eating. No one has ever seen a real one climb a tall building.

---

1. about 15 meters   3. almost 2 meters
2. almost 2½ meters   4. about 181 kilograms

If King Kong wasn't real, how did movie makers make him appear real? They built a small model with parts that moved. They would take one picture of the model. Then they would move the model a fraction of an inch and take another picture. King Kong looked as if he were moving. But "giant" King Kong was really sixteen inches tall.[1]

Sharpen Your Skills

When you read, you often learn how two things are like or different from each other.

1. How was the size that King Kong looked different from the size of a real gorilla?
2. King Kong was fierce. Are real gorillas fierce like King Kong or different from King Kong?

When you read the next two articles, look for how movie monsters are like real animals and people yet different from them.

---

1. about $40\frac{1}{2}$ centimeters

Movie Monsters: Are They for Real?

by Phil Bowkett

Would *Jaws* scare *you*?

The scare you get in a good monster movie is real. But how real is the movie monster itself?

Some are based on real animals. The shark in the 1975 movie *Jaws* was based on a white shark. A white shark is about 20 to 25 feet[1] long. The heaviest one ever caught weighed about 7,000 pounds.[2] The fish in *Jaws* was 25 feet[3] long and weighed 2,000 pounds.[4] A white shark swims easily. But it took fifteen people to move the fish in *Jaws* through the water.

Two sharks were made for *Jaws*. One was made to be pulled through the water. The other was placed on a platform. Both could move their tails from side to side. Most importantly, both could bite and chew.

1. 6 to 7½ meters   3. 7½ meters
2. 3 metric tons   4. 1 metric ton

In *The Creature from the Black Lagoon,* made in 1954, the monster was based on three different animals. It had the head of a fish, the hands and feet of a frog, and a scaly body like an alligator.

The monster was played by a man wearing a special suit. The man inside could swim and fight like a person, but he looked like a very strange animal.

The monster starts to climb onto a boat.

Millicent Patrick thought up the monster's mask.

There is nothing on earth quite like Godzilla. He first appeared in 1954. He was made by movie makers in Japan.

Godzilla is taller than the highest building. He's green and scaly. He destroys whole cities with his huge feet and tail. He breathes fire.

Perhaps the closest real animal to Godzilla was one of the dinosaurs. It was a huge animal that ate meat. But it didn't breathe fire, and we don't know what color it was.

Godzilla was brought to life in two ways. In some portions of the movie, a person dressed up in a monster suit. In other portions, Godzilla was only a small model.

Sometimes Godzilla looks very real. At other times he doesn't. But it doesn't matter. Audiences have a great time. They love being scared by such a terrible monster!

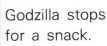

Godzilla stops for a snack.

That Face— That Beautiful Face

by M. H. Novak

There aren't many people who think that monsters are beautiful. But the people who plan the makeup for movie monsters do. Makeup artists turn real people into monsters.

One of the best-known movie monsters of all time was made more than fifty years ago. In 1931 Boris Karloff played the monster in the movie *Frankenstein*. Karloff was a very nice-looking, quiet man. When the makeup artist had finished with him, Karloff would have frightened his own family.

The man who changed Karloff into a monster was Jack Pierce. It took Pierce three months just to think up the plan for Karloff's makeup.

Pierce changed the shape of Karloff's head so that it was square and flat. He put blue-green paint on Karloff's face. That made him look pale in the black-and-white movie. Then bolts were attached to Karloff's neck. They were supposed to show where the monster was hooked up to Dr. Frankenstein's machine.

Pierce put metal poles in the legs of Karloff's pants. They made Karloff walk with a very stiff motion. Then Pierce gave Karloff heavy boots to wear. He also put padding around Karloff's body so that it looked bigger and heavier than it really was.

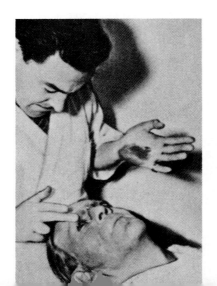

While the movie was being made, Karloff had to be made up every morning. It took over three hours to get his makeup on, so he had to start at 5:30 A.M.

Boris Karloff always praised Jack Pierce for his great makeup job. Karloff said he felt it was Pierce who made the monster. But both men had to work together. Pierce made the monster look frightening. Karloff's acting made it come alive.

Checking Comprehension and Skills

1. What three monsters were discussed in "Movie Monsters: Are They For Real?"

•2. What real animals were these three movie monsters based on? How was each monster like the real animal? How was each monster different from the real animal?

•3. Which monster in "Movie Monsters" is most like the monster in "That Face—That Beautiful Face"? How are they alike?

4. Who were Boris Karloff and Jack Pierce? (421-422)

5. Read the last paragraph on page 423. Which sentence states the main idea? In what way is that sentence true?

•6. Which of the monsters in this unit was most frightening to you? Why?

7. Think of the scariest monster you can. What does it look like? What does it sound like? How does it move?

Which word would you use in this sentence?
○8. The robot moved with a slow, stiff ____.
portion   nation   motion

• Comparative relationships
○ Structure: Syllables

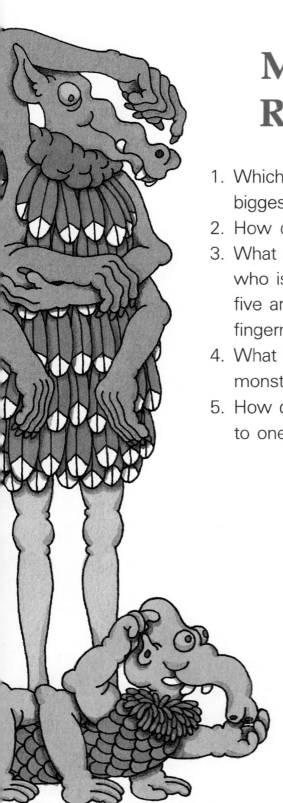

Monster Riddles!

JUST FOR YOU

1. Which monsters wear the biggest shoes?
2. How does a monster begin?
3. What do you call a monster who is ten feet tall and has five arms and poison fingernails?
4. What time is it when a monster sits on a clock?
5. How does a monster count to one hundred?

Answers:
1. The ones with the biggest feet.
2. With the letter *m*.
3. Anything it wants to be called.
4. Time to get a new clock.
5. On its fingers.

Look It Over

Can you find the monster in the picture? Look the crowd over until you spot it.

You often look things over quickly to find the one thing you are looking for. When you read, you might look over the selection quickly to find one piece of information. That is called **skimming.**

When you skim, look for a key word or number. Look over the selection quickly until you find it. Then slow down and read that part of the selection until you have all your information.

Skim pages 421 to 423 to find out how long it took to put on Karloff's makeup. Don't forget—you can skim anything you read.

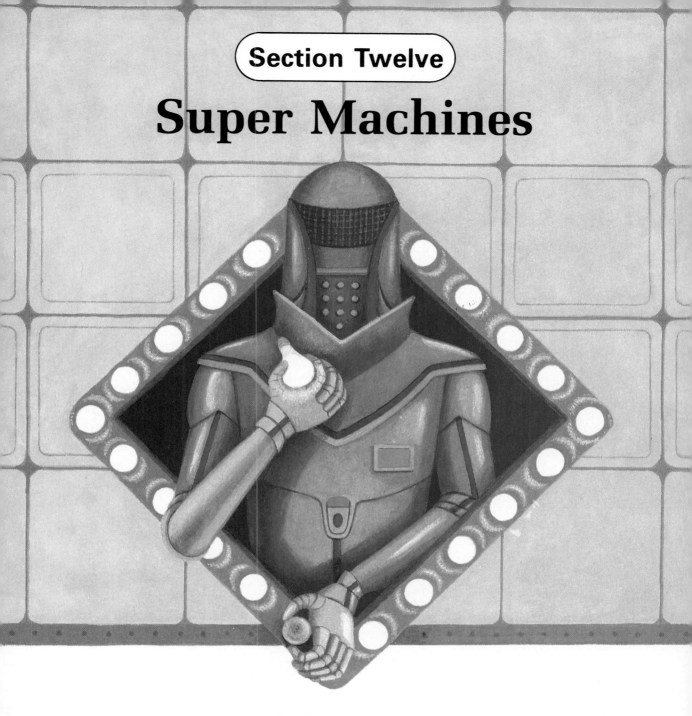

Section Twelve
Super Machines

KEEP
A
412
SELECT
READY
TAPE INDICATE
LOAD REWIND
START
UNLOAD REWIND
RESET

What Is a Computer?

A computer is a machine. It can keep a lot of information on file. It can do many kinds of problems and answer many questions. It can do these things very quickly. But the machine has to be told what to do and how to use the information.

A person tells the computer what to do through a *program*. This is every single step that must be used to solve a problem. If the person makes even one small mistake, the machine will make mistakes.

What a Computer Can Do

by Henry Larson

A computer can do many kinds of math problems. How quickly can it do them? One of the first computers was made in 1944. It could do about five multiplications in one second. Computers can now do millions of multiplications in a second.

Because these machines are fast and exact, they are used in many ways. For example, they must be used to make a rocket work exactly right. In food stores, they keep track of what has been sold and what is left to be sold. Doctors use them to figure out the results of tests.

More uses are being found all the time for computers.

Your Computer, Your Dog, and You

by Matthew Yuen

A computer is dumb—really dumb. Yes, it does problems faster than you can think them. Yes, it remembers a lot of things you tell it. But it's not "smart." It just obeys.

If something can *do* a few things better than you can,

that doesn't make it *better* than you. Even your dog can probably run faster, jump higher, and hear better than you can. It can probably remember where it buried your slippers long after you've forgotten all about them. But that doesn't make your dog smarter than you. After all, how can you call an animal that eats dog food, and loves it, smarter than you? And how can you call a machine that sleeps all day—until you wake it up— smart? Even your dog wakes up without your help.

Sharpen Your Skills

An author usually has a **purpose,** one main reason for writing. The author may want to inform you, entertain you, or persuade you.
1. Does the first article's author want to inform you with facts or entertain you with funny ideas? Why do you think as you do?
2. What is the second author's purpose?

As you read the next stories, try to figure out what purpose each author had for writing.

What Can You Do with a Computer?

by Marilyn Sherman

Four ten-year-old boys and girls sprawl on the living room rug. They face a screen, talk, and laugh. Suddenly they cheer.

What would cause them to do this? They are using a computer! Soon machines like theirs may become as common in homes as telephones or radios.

Home computers are small but powerful. How can families use them? In many families, young people like you use them the most.

The hardest thing about using a home computer is programming it. When you program it, you make it do what you want it to do. You can make it work real problems. You can make up new games. You can even write your own songs. You can also program a home computer to make pictures. Then you can make the pictures move or change colors.

You can use your home computer to learn many kinds of school subjects. It can make learning more fun. It can tell stories. (Some of these machines can even make sounds!) It can even help you write reports.

Using one can also make many hobbies more fun. Do you like sports? You can keep track of the records of the team or players you like best. Are you a collector? You can keep lists of what you own. Do you like to build things? You can use the computer to help you plan what to build.

A home computer can also save work around the house. It can help your family plan meals. It can help your family plan how to save or spend money. Soon your family may use it to shop and send messages too.

Young people like you are spending more and more time with home computers. As you do, you will find even more uses for them. And you will find that you are also using your own mind. You can have fun when computers make you think!

Such a Nice Little Planet

from a cartoon by Suzan Jarvis

The family was resting after a dinner of raw rocks. Their orange skin glowed in the light of the three moons.

"Well, family, where shall we go on our vacation this year?" asked Father.

"Oh, please, let's not go to Planet J516 again this year," begged Son.

"I agree," said Daughter, sprawled out on the floor. "Learning to ride the giant bats there was fun. But that place is too far away. I got rocket-sick on the way home."

"I have an idea," said Mother. "Let's ask the computer. Maybe it knows a good place."

435

They all walked over to a small box on the table. Mother tapped the box with a claw. "Computer," she said, "we want you to help us find an interesting place to visit. You listen while each of us tells you what we want. I want to go somewhere that doesn't have a green sky like ours. It's so dull."

"I'm tired of pink ground," Son yawned.

"I want to go some place that no one in our city has ever visited," said Father.

"And I don't want to go too far. No more than twelve trillion miles," added Daughter.

"All right, Computer. What can you come up with?" Mother asked. She was so excited that her eye was wide open.

"I know just the place for you," it answered. "The sky is blue. The ground is brown with green on it. It is only nine trillion miles away. No one from our planet has ever been there. And," it added, "you could go swimming."

"Swimming? What's swimming?" asked Son.

"The beings on this planet like to jump into large bodies of water and flap their arms around," answered the computer.

"That sounds like fun to me," Mother decided. "But, Computer, if it is so nice, why does no one go there for vacations?"

"Oh . . . I don't know," it answered.

"Computer, you must tell us everything. It will be your fault if we have a bad time. You know we can unplug you," Father said.

"All right! All right," it answered. "The beings there have two eyes."

"Two eyes! How awful!" Father screamed.

"How disgusting!" Son and Daughter cried.

"Computer, that will never do. We could not stand the sight of anything so ugly," said Mother.

"Too bad," the computer sighed. "Earth is such a nice little planet, overall."

437

Checking Comprehension and Skills

1. What is the hardest thing about using a computer? (432)

•2. Did the author of "What Can You Do with a Computer?" mostly want to inform you with facts and ideas, entertain you with funny ideas, or persuade you to do something? Why do you think as you do?

3. How would you use a computer in your home?

4. How did the family in "Such a Nice Little Planet" use its computer? (436-437)

•5. Did the author of the story mostly want to inform you, entertain you, or persuade you about something? Why do you think so?

6. The family thought that beings with two eyes were ugly. Why is that a funny idea?

Which word would you use in each sentence?

○7. It was the dog's ___ that the dish broke.
   fall   far   fault

○8. This hamburger isn't cooked; it's ___.
   raw   ran   raisin

○9. My sister was so tired she ___.
   yet   yard   yawned

• Author's purpose
○ Phonics: Vowels (au/ô/, aw/ô/)

Can a Calculator Talk?

A calculator is really a tiny computer. And, yes, a calculator can talk to you!

1. Press these keys: 14. Turn the calculator upside down. Do you see it saying "hi" to you?

2. Say to the calculator, "When water gets very hot, what does it do?" Press the keys 57108 and turn it upside down. (Yes, water boils!)

3. Ask, "What do plants need besides light, air, and water?" Press the keys 7105 and turn the calculator upside down. (Right again! Plants need soil.)

4. If it can answer questions, it must be very smart. Ask it, "Do I work for you or am I the boss?" Press the keys 5508 and turn it upside down. (See? It knows!)

What other words can you get it to say?

A Computer That Moves

A robot is a machine that can move in order to do a job. A computer makes the machine work. People program the computer. Then it tells the robot what parts to move and when to move them.

Many people think that all robots look like people, with arms and legs and a head. Robots in movies and some in real life are shaped like people. But many companies now use robots that do not look like people at all. These machines do jobs that people can also do. They have a shape that has been made just for the job they have to do.

Using What You Know

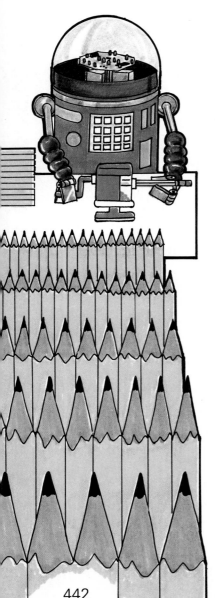

You can think of many ways to use a robot. You also know many ways to figure out new words.

Sharpen Your Skills

Here are several ways you've learned to figure out words.

- **Sense and consonants** Think of a word you know that makes sense in the sentence. Then see if the consonants in your word match the consonants in the new word. Can you read the sentence below?

    The robot did many jobs for the cl_ss, like handing out books.

- **Root words** Sometimes a word may look strange because it is a root word with a prefix, suffix, or ending added to it. Can you read the underlined words below?

    We also used the robot to <u>unpack</u> <u>boxes</u> and <u>sharpen</u> pencils.

- **Syllables** Another way you know to figure out a word is to break it into syllables. Figure out the parts, then put the parts together again. Where do you break the underlined words in this sentence?

  In a blizzard, a clever robot gets snow off the walk before you hurt your ankle.

- **Meaning** Sometimes you may be able to read a word but not know what it means. Use the meaning of the words around the unknown word to figure out what it means. Can you figure out what trundled means below?

  The robot trundled a shopping cart full of food. It pushed the cart slowly.

Use one or more of these ways to figure out the underlined words below.

Mary saw an ad for the Robot Cook. This robot fixes meals faster than you can wink your eye. The Robot Cook bakes tasty rolls and muffins that make your mouth water. If this robot ever burns a dinner, the company will give you a refund of the money you paid.

Use what you know to figure out words the next time you read.

Why You Need a Robot

by
O. B. Hawker

Do you need a robot? Of course you do! What could one do for you? It could clean your room for you. It could wash your dishes. It could answer your phone. It could meet people at the door for you. It could take your dog for a walk. It could do some of the dull work that you don't like to do. You will think of many ways a robot could help you. You will see that you can hardly get along without one.

If none of your neighbors has a robot, think of how good you would feel to have one! Everyone would want to see it. They would want to watch it work. They might want to use it for a while. You might even meet some new friends if you had a robot.

Sharpen Your Skills

An **author's purpose** for writing may be to entertain you, to inform you, or to persuade you. When the main purpose is to persuade you, the author wants you to act or think in a certain way. For example, the author of an ad may want you to buy a certain product, to vote for a certain person, or to watch a certain TV show.

1. The author of this article is trying to persuade you of something. What is it?
2. What are two ideas that the author uses to try to persuade you?

Notice how the ads try to persuade the family in "If Not Totally Satisfied."

If Not Totally Satisfied

by
Sharon Fear

"What this family needs," said Dad, "is a robot."

Mom, Dad, and I had just been talking about how busy we were. Dad said he didn't have time to cut the grass. He was trying to get me to do it. But I had a violin lesson and work for school to finish.

We looked hopefully at Mom. "Not me," she said. "After I finish the article I'm writing, I have some housework to do."

So when Dad said "robot" my eyes popped. Mom, though, got that look on her face that always means she is not sure.

"It's the coming thing," Dad said. "Why, twenty years ago only a few people had their own computers. Now everybody has one. And look at this." He opened the newspaper to show us an ad.

"It sounds helpful," said Mom. "But—"

"Now here's something I could use," said Dad, showing us another ad.

"Oh, look!" I yelled. I showed them the ad *I* had just found in a magazine.

In fact, the picture of a robot in a clown suit was really funny. We almost rolled on the floor laughing. But we decided that none of these seemed quite right. Each could only do one kind of work. Maybe a robot wasn't for us. Secretly, though, I hadn't given up the idea.

Ten days later I thought I had the answer. I had found another ad. I took it to Mom and Dad. I just knew that they would like it.

You need

H.E.L.P.,

and we can give it to you.

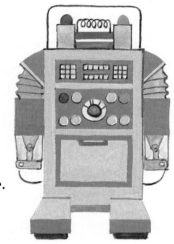

H.E.L.P. is truly the best in robot help around the house. Choose programs for cooking, child care, cleaning, lawn and garden care, fun, learning, and much more.

To learn more, call the helpful people at

H.E.L.P.

Videophone 3139-0-5465

If not totally satisfied,
your money will be returned.

"The ad makes it sound like this robot can do just about anything," said Dad.

"It must cost a lot," said Mom.

"But," I said, "notice that you can get your money back if you are not satisfied."

"All right," said Mom. "Let's call."

So we did. One of H.E.L.P.'s helpful people came to our home. She talked to us about their robots. We liked what we saw and heard. We had one sent to us that very day.

The next morning each of us programmed H.E.L.P. to do some of our jobs. Then we all went to the park for a ball game.

When we came back and walked up to our house, we saw that something was awfully wrong. All over the lawn little clumps of grass had been pulled up. Mom pointed to where the vacuum cleaner, broken and filled up with grass, lay near the front door.

"I programmed H.E.L.P. to vacuum the carpet!" she cried.

"I told it to mow the lawn!" said Dad.

"It must have vacuumed the lawn," I said. "If it did that, it must have—"

"MOWED THE CARPET!" we all cried at the same time.

We dashed inside. Sure enough, our carpet, which used to be deep and thick, was now just a thin sheet of cloth.

"What is that strange smell?" asked Dad.

"I programmed H.E.L.P. to bake some bread," said Mom. "But that's not bread."

"Oh no!" I groaned and shook my head. "I programmed it to tune my violin!"

We got to the kitchen just as H.E.L.P. took my smoking violin out of the oven. Later I checked my violin case. Sure enough, there I found the bread dough.

As you might think, we were not totally satisfied! We returned our robot and got our money back.

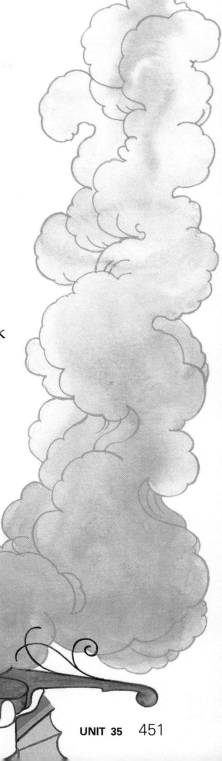

Checking Comprehension and Skills

1. What did the family in this story want? How did they get what they wanted?
2. Choose the sentence that sums up the story:
   a. H.E.L.P. put the violin in the oven and put bread dough in the violin case.
   b. The family thought a robot would help them, but the robot got mixed up and caused many problems.
●3. Did the companies who had ads in this story mainly want to inform with facts, entertain with funny ideas, or persuade the readers to do something? Why do you think that?
●4. How is the ad for ROY on page 447 different from the other ads in this story?
5. The ad for H.E.L.P. said that this robot was the "best in robot help around the house." What would the family in this story say about that statement, and why?
6. How do you think the family felt about ads and robots at the end of the story?

   Which word would you use in this sentence?
○7. She is ____ my best friend.
   truth   truly   trick

   ● Author's purpose   ○ Word Study Strategies

Stop for a Robot

by Eve Bunting

Pam and Kerry are twins whose mother gave them a robot for their birthday. The twins' mother and the high-school class she taught had made it. Its eyes flash, and it can walk. It can speak the words that are put on its tape. The twins have had a lot of fun with Robot. Now Mom, Pam, and Kerry are getting ready to go visit the children's grandparents.

"Robot won't fit in the car," Mom said. "I'll have to take him apart."

"Do you have to?" Kerry asked.

Robot was like a person now. It was hard to watch Mom taking off his legs and arms and head.

Mom stored him in a box that would fit in the trunk. Kerry wished Robot could at least be inside the car, but there was no room. Their car was pretty small. It had to hold Mom, Pam, and Kerry himself, and all the birthday gifts they were taking to Grandma.

Kerry tried not to think about the robot in bits in the trunk. He thought about seeing Grandma and Grandpa and all their old friends again.

"Better Robot in the trunk than Robot left behind," Pam said.

It was raining hard. The drops pattered on the car roof. The wipers swished. It was hard driving for Mom. But the car was warm and dry inside.

They were out of the town now. Tonight they would stay in a motel. Mom turned onto a side road, and they drove on and on.

"Here's the river," Mom said at last.

The car lights shone on the wet road. The bridge railings were rusty red.

Kerry peered out the window. "Can you see the water yet, Pam?" he asked. But Pam was asleep in the back seat.

All at once Mom slammed on the brakes. Kerry bumped against the door. His seat belt cut into his middle. The car's wheels skidded. The car slid sideways and stopped.

Pam was suddenly wide awake. "Mom! What's wrong?" she yelled.

The wipers hissed across the glass. Kerry could hear the sound of the river and the sound of his own heart beating. "What happened, Mom?" he asked.

"The bridge," she said. "It's not there."

Kerry looked out the side window. There was only black space.

"The bridge got washed away," Mom said.

Kerry felt sick. What if Mom hadn't seen?

"Let's go back," Pam said.

Mom nodded and said, "We'll call the police." She started the car. Then she turned the motor off again. "We can't just go," she said. "What if another car comes? What if the driver doesn't see and can't stop in time?"

"I know," Kerry said. "We can put flares across the road."

"I don't think I have any," Mom said. She found a flashlight in the car, but its beam was weak.

"I can shine the car's lights on the river," Mom said. "That will help."

"Sure," said Kerry, and he tried to sound sure. "I'll see if there's anything in the trunk," he said. He didn't add "like a few old flares."

He saw the robot as soon as he opened the trunk, and he had an idea. "Mom," he called. "Can you come here?"

Pam and Mom came quickly. They all stood in the rain looking in the open trunk.

"Could you put Robot back the way he was?" Kerry asked. "Real, real fast?"

Mom stared at him. "Kerry! That's a great idea!"

Mom got her tools from the toolbox. Pam helped her with Robot while Kerry watched for cars. Mom tried to hurry. The rain made her hands wet. The tools kept slipping. Now Robot's legs were on. Now his arms were on—and now his head. Mom checked his wires. She took the control box.

Kerry held his breath. What if Mom had goofed up on something?

Robot's eye lights beamed on. He moved. He was all right!

Mom walked him to the place where the bridge used to be. She put new words on his tape. Then Mom moved the car. She turned on the car lights so that they shone on the robot. Then the family sat in the car with the control box. Mom pressed Voice On and turned the sound to High. Robot's voice boomed out: "Danger. The bridge is down. Stop your car."

"They should really hear that!" Pam said.

They waited in the car and waited and waited. Finally Mom said, "Here comes something."

Car lights were coming fast. Pam and Kerry got out and waved their arms. The robot's big voice filled the night.

The car slowed and stopped. Pam and Kerry ran up to it. A man and a woman sat inside. Kerry told them what had happened.

The man's voice was shaky when he spoke. "It's a good thing that robot is so big and shiny. The roads are so slick that it's hard to see. But I saw him all right."

The man had a box of flares. They spread the flares ahead of Robot.

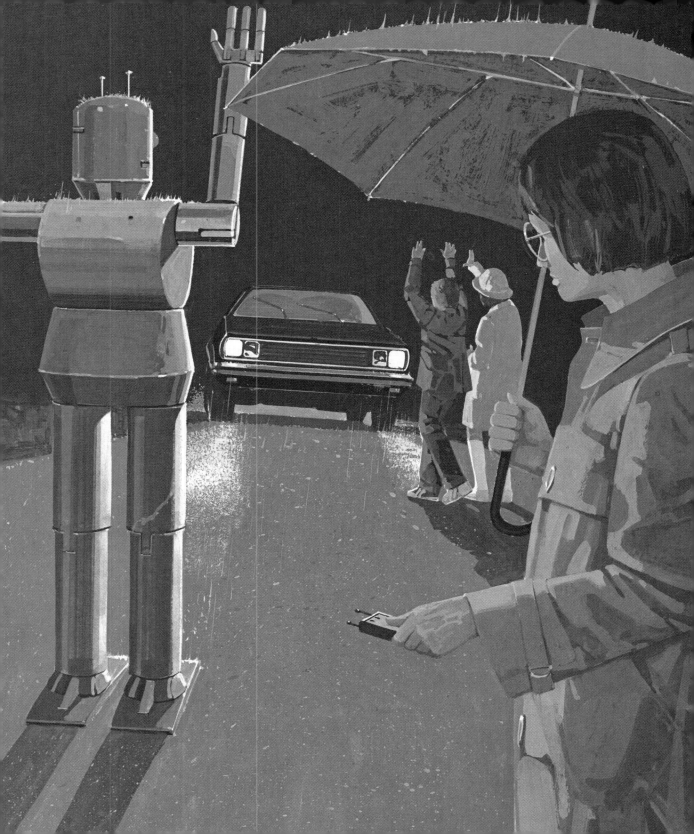

"I'll drive back to a phone," the man said. "But can the robot stay where he is? Anyone will stop for a robot."

"Yes," Mom said. "Please hurry."

Mom, Pam, and Kerry kept watch. Robot had to stop two more cars. Both drivers had flares.

"They're smart to have flares," Mom said.

"They didn't make a robot," Kerry said proudly. "You're smarter than anyone."

Mom messed up his hair, smiling, and said, "No. People are just smart in different ways. And dumb in different ways too."

They heard police sirens far, far away.

"Will we still get to go to Grandma's?" Pam asked.

"We'll have to go the long way," Mom answered. "But we'll still make it in time for Grandma's birthday!"

Books to Read

Crinkleroot's Guide to Walking in Wild Places
by Jim Arnosky

Crinkleroot says he was born in a tree and raised by bees. His funny book tells you how to have fun safely as you walk outdoors in the fields and woods.

The Dragonling
by Jackie French Koller

By chance, Darek finds a baby dragon left alive after its mother is killed by the people of his village. Darek risks death and the anger of his people when he decides to return the dragonling to the Valley of the Dragons.

Look at Color and Camouflage
by Rachel Wright

Some animals play tricks by changing their color or shape. See how animals do this to fool their enemies and live another day.

Glossary

How to Use the Pronunciation Key

After each entry word in this glossary, there is a special spelling, called the **pronunciation.** It shows how to say the word. The word is broken into syllables and then spelled with letters and signs. You can look up these letters and signs in the **pronunciation key** to see what sounds they stand for.

This dark mark (′) is called the **primary accent.** It follows the syllable you say with the most force. This lighter mark (′) is the **secondary accent.** Say the syllable it follows with medium force. Syllables without marks are said with least force.

Full Pronunciation Key

a	hat, cap	**i**	it, pin	**p**	paper, cup	**z**	zoo, breeze
ā	age, face	**ī**	ice, five	**r**	run, try	**zh**	measure, seizure
ä	father, far			**s**	say, yes		
		j	jam, enjoy	**sh**	she, rush	**ə**	represents:
b	bad, rob	**k**	kind, seek	**t**	tell, it		a in about
ch	child, much	**l**	land, coal	**th**	thin, both		e in taken
d	did, red	**m**	me, am	**ᴛʜ**	then, smooth		i in pencil
		n	no, in				o in lemon
e	let, best	**ng**	long, bring	**u**	cup, butter		u in circus
ē	equal, be			**ủ**	full, put		
ėr	her, learn	**o**	hot, rock	**ü**	rule, move		
		ō	open, go				
f	fat, if	**ô**	order, all	**v**	very, save		
g	go, bag	**oi**	oil, toy	**w**	will, woman		
h	he, how	**ou**	house, out	**y**	young, yet		

The contents of the Glossary entries in this book have been adapted from *My Second Picture Dictionary,* Copyright © 1982 Scott, Foresman and Company; *Scott, Foresman Beginning Dictionary,* Copyright © 1983 Scott, Foresman and Company; *Scott, Foresman Intermediate Dictionary,* Copyright © 1983 Scott, Foresman and Company; and *Scott, Foresman Advanced Dictionary,* Copyright © 1983 Scott, Foresman and Company.

A a

ac·ci·dent (ak'sə dənt), something harmful or unlucky that happens: *She was hurt in an automobile accident. noun.*

Af·ri·ca (af'rə kə), one of the large masses of land on the earth; a continent. See picture. *noun.*

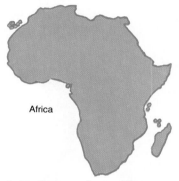

Africa

a·lone (ə lōn'), apart from other persons or things: *After the children left, the teacher was alone in the school. adjective.*

an·chor (ang'kər), a heavy piece of iron or steel fastened to a chain or rope and dropped from a ship to the bottom of the water to hold the ship in place. See picture. *noun.*

anchor

an·noy (ə noi'), make somewhat angry; disturb or trouble someone: *The baby is always annoying his sister by pulling her hair. verb.*

arc·tic (ärk'tik *or* är'tik), **1** at or near the North Pole. **2 the Arctic,** the north polar

a hat	i it	oi oil	ch child	(a in about
ā age	ī ice	ou out	ng long	e in taken
ä far	o hot	u cup	sh she	ə = { i in pencil
e let	ō open	ů put	th thin	o in lemon
ē equal	ô order	ü rule	ᵮH then	(u in circus
ėr term			zh measure	

region. The Arctic has a very cold winter. **1** *adjective,* **2** *noun.*

ar·e·a (er'ē ə *or* ar'ē ə), **1** amount of surface: *The area of this floor is 600 square feet.* **2** region: *The Rocky Mountain area is the most mountainous in the United States. noun.*

ar·my (är'mē), a large group of soldiers trained for war: *American armies have fought in many lands. noun, plural* **ar·mies.**

ar·ti·cle (är'tə kəl), a piece of writing that is part of a magazine, newspaper, or book: *This is a good article on gardening. noun.*

B b

ban·jo (ban'jō), a musical instrument having four or five strings, played by plucking the strings with the fingers or a pick. See picture. *noun, plural* **ban·jos.**

banjo

463

bare (ber *or* bar), without covering; not covered: *The top of the hill was bare.* adjective, **bar·er, bar·est.**

bay[1] (bā), part of a sea or lake reaching into the land. *noun.*

bay[2] (bā), a long, deep barking, usually by a large dog: *We heard the distant bay of the hounds.* noun.

bed·roll (bed'rōl'), blankets that can be rolled up and tied for carrying. *noun.*

bi·cy·cle (bī'sik'əl), a vehicle with two wheels, one behind the other. You ride it by pushing two pedals. See picture. *noun.*

bicycle

bit·ter (bit'ər), sharp; biting; very cold: *The bitter winter killed our apple tree.* adjective.

blend (blend), mix together; shade into each other, little by little: *The colors of the rainbow blend into one another.* verb.

bliz·zard (bliz'ərd), a blinding snowstorm with a very strong wind and very great cold. *noun.*

board (bôrd), a broad, thin piece of wood for use in building: *We used boards 10 inches wide and 10 feet long.* noun.

bolt (bōlt), rod with a head at one end and a screw thread for a nut at the other. Bolts are used to fasten things together or hold something in place. See picture. *noun.*

boom (büm), make a deep hollow sound: *His voice boomed out above the rest.* verb.

brace (brās), **1** thing that holds parts together or in place, such as pieces of wood used to make a building stronger or a metal frame to hold the ankle straight: *The brace kept the wall from falling.* **2** prepare (oneself): *He braced himself for the crash.* 1 *noun,* 2 *verb.*

braid (brād), **1** a kind of band or rope made by weaving together hair, ribbon, or flowers. **2** weave together hair, ribbon, or flowers. See picture. 1 *noun,* 2 *verb.*

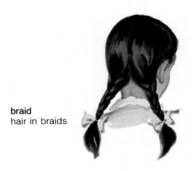

braid
hair in braids

brass (bras), a yellowish metal that is made of copper and zinc. *noun.*

breathe (brēŧH), draw air into the lungs and force it out. You breathe through your nose or through your mouth. *verb,* **breathed, breath·ing.**

bur·row (bėr'ō), **1** hole dug in the ground by an animal. Rabbits live in burrows. **2** dig a hole in the ground: *The mole was burrowing in our back yard.* 1 *noun,* 2 *verb.*

buz·zard (buz'ərd), a large, heavy, slow-moving hawk. *noun.*

BOLT   NUT
bolt

C c

a hat	**i** it	**oi** oil	**ch** child	⎧ a in about
ā age	**ī** ice	**ou** out	**ng** long	⎪ e in taken
ä far	**o** hot	**u** cup	**sh** she	**ə** = ⎨ i in pencil
e let	**ō** open	**ù** put	**th** thin	⎪ o in lemon
ē equal	**ô** order	**ü** rule	**ŦH** then	⎩ u in circus
ėr term			**zh** measure	

cal·cu·late (kal′kyə lāt), find out by adding, subtracting, multiplying, or dividing. *verb.* **cal·cu·lat·ed, cal·cu·lat·ing.**

cal·cu·la·tor (kal′kyə lā′tər), machine that calculates; machine that solves arithmetic problems. *noun.*

Cal·i·for·nia (kal′ə fôr′nyə), one of the Pacific Coast states of the United States. See picture. *noun.*

California

Sacramento

camp (kamp), a place outside or a group of tents or huts where people live for a while: *We set up camp near the river. noun.*

camp·ground (kamp′ground′), a place, usually a park, where people can camp. *noun.*

Can·a·da (kan′ə də), country in North America, north of the United States. See picture. *noun.*

cause (kôz), make happen; bring about: *The fire caused much damage to the building. A loud noise caused me to jump. verb,* **caused, caus·ing.**

ceil·ing (sē′ling), the inside, top covering of a room. *noun.*

cem·e·ter·y (sem′ə ter′ē), place for burying the dead. *noun, plural* **cem·e·ter·ies.**

Central America, part of North America between Mexico and South America.

chirp (chėrp), make a short, sharp sound: *The crickets chirped outside the house. verb.*

chuck·le (chuk′əl), laugh softly or quietly: *She chuckled to herself. verb,* **chuck·led, chuck·ling.**

coast (kōst), land along the sea; the seashore. See picture. *noun.*

coast

CANADA

Ottawa

Canada

coin|dentist

coin (koin), a piece of metal made by the government for use as money. Pennies, nickels, dimes, and quarters are coins. *noun.*

col·lapse (kə laps'), fall down; break down suddenly: *Sticking a pin into the balloon caused it to collapse. She collapsed on the sofa. verb.* **col·lapsed, col·laps·ing.**

col·lect (kə lekt'), bring together; gather together: *I collect stamps as a hobby. verb.*

col·lec·tor (kə lek'tər), person who collects: *I am a stamp collector. noun.*

com·pute (kəm pyüt'), do by arithmetic; count; figure out. *verb,* **com·put·ed, com·put·ing.**

com·put·er (kəm pyü'tər), machine which computes, solves problems, and stores up information. *noun.*

con·vince (kən vins'), make a person feel sure; cause to believe: *The mistakes she made convinced me that she had not studied her lesson. verb,* **con·vinced, con·vinc·ing.**

coun·try (kun'trē), 1 land; a certain area. See picture. 2 all the land of a nation: *France is a country in Europe.* 3 land where a person was born or where he or she is a citizen: *The United States is my country. noun, plural* **coun·tries.**

country (definition 1)

cov·er·all (kuv'ər ôl'). Often, **coveralls,** *plural,* work clothing made with the shirt and trousers in a single piece. *noun.*

crash (krash), the noisy striking of one solid thing against another: *There was a crash of two cars at the corner. noun.*

crick·et (krik'it), a black insect something like a grasshopper. Male crickets make a noise by rubbing their front wings together. See picture. *noun.*

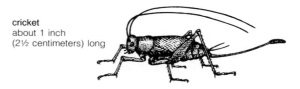

cricket
about 1 inch
(2½ centimeters) long

crop (krop), plants grown for people to use: *Wheat, corn, and cotton are three crops of the United States. noun.*

curve (kėrv), bend in a road: *The automobile had to slow down to go around the curves. noun.*

D d

dawn (dôn), the beginning of day; the first light in the east: *In summer dawn comes early. noun.*

den·tist (den'tist), a person whose business is caring for people's teeth. See picture. *noun.*

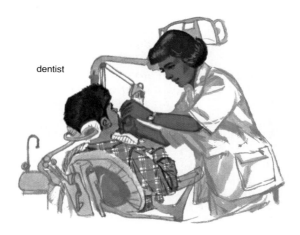

dentist

de·pressed (di prest'), gloomy; sad: *The rain made us depressed.* adjective.

dis·ap·pear (dis'ə pir'), be gone or lost; stop being: *When spring comes, the snow disappears.* verb.

dis·cov·er·y (dis kuv'ər ē), a finding out; a seeing or learning of something for the first time. *noun, plural* **dis·cov·er·ies.**

ditch

ditch (dich), a long, narrow place dug in the earth. Ditches are usually used to carry off water. See picture. *noun, plural* **ditch·es.**

dough (dō), a soft, thick mixture of flour, liquid, and other things from which bread, biscuits, cake, and pie crust are made. *noun.*

driz·zle (driz'əl), very small drops of rain like mist: *A steady drizzle made it hard to see across the muddy football field.* noun.

dull (dul), **1** not sharp or pointed: *It is hard to cut with a dull knife.* **2** not interesting; tiresome; boring: *a dull book.* adjective.

a hat	i it	oi oil	ch child	(a in about
ā age	ī ice	ou out	ng long	e in taken
ä far	o hot	u cup	sh she	ə = { i in pencil
e let	ō open	ů put	th thin	o in lemon
ē equal	ô order	ü rule	ŦH then	(u in circus
er term			zh measure	

en·e·my (en'ə mē), **1** animal, person, or group that hates or tries to harm another. Two countries fighting against each other are enemies. **2** anything that will harm: *Frost is an enemy of flowers.* noun, plural **en·e·mies.**

es·cape (e skāp'), get free or get out and away: *The bird escaped from its cage.* verb, **es·caped, es·cap·ing.**

eve·ning (ēv'ning), the time between sunset and bedtime: *Jim often spends the evening reading a good book.* noun.

ex·am·ple (eg zam'pəl), one thing taken to show what the others are like: *New York is an example of a busy city.* noun.

ex·pla·na·tion (ek'splə nā'shən), something that makes plain; something that clears up a question or a mistake: *He did not understand the teacher's explanation of multiplication.* noun.

ex·plo·sion (ek splō'zhən), a sudden blowing up; a sudden bursting forth: *explosions of laughter; explosions of color.* noun.

E e

em·pire (em'pīr), a group of nations or states under one ruler or government. *noun.*

emp·ty (emp'tē), not real; without meaning; with nothing to it: *An empty promise is one that you do not plan to keep.* adjective, **emp·ti·er, emp·ti·est.**

F f

face (fās), to have the front toward: *The house faces the street.* verb.

farm·land (färm'land'), land used for raising crops or as pasture for animals. *noun.*

fierce (firs), wild; ready to fight: *A wounded lion can be fierce.* adjective, **fierc·er, fierc·est.**

flare (fler *or* flar), a light that burns for a short time, used for signaling. *noun.*

flop (flop), **1** move loosely or heavily; flap around clumsily: *The fish flopped helplessly on the deck.* **2** fall, drop, or move heavily or clumsily: *The tired girl flopped down into a chair. verb,* **flopped, flop·ping.**

Flo·ri·da (flôr′ə də), one of the southeastern states of the United States. See picture. *noun.*

Florida

flus·ter (flus′tər), make nervous and upset; make excited; confuse: *The honking of horns flustered the driver, and he stalled his automobile. verb.*

fork (fôrk), one of the branches into which anything is divided. See picture. *noun.*

fork—fork in road

for·tune (fôr′chən), a great deal of money or property; riches: *The family made a fortune in oil. noun.*

fos·sil (fos′əl), the traces of an animal or plant of long ago, turned into stone. Fossils of ferns are sometimes found in coal. See picture. *noun.*

fossil

fun·nel (fun′l), a tube with a wide, cone-shaped mouth, or anything shaped in this way. See picture. *noun.*

funnel

fu·ture (fyü′chər), the time to come; what is to come: *You cannot change the past, but you can do better in the future. noun.*

G g

Ga·lá·pa·gos Islands (gə lä′pə gəs *or* gə lä′pə gōs), group of islands in the Pacific Ocean off the west coast of South America.

gear (gir), wheel having teeth that fit into teeth in another wheel; wheels turning one another by teeth. If the wheels are of different sizes they will turn at different speeds. See picture. *noun.*

gears

a hat	**i** it	**oi** oil	**ch** child	⎧ a in about
ā age	**ī** ice	**ou** out	**ng** long	e in taken
ä far	**o** hot	**u** cup	**sh** she ə =	i in pencil
e let	**ō** open	**ù** put	**th** thin	o in lemon
ē equal	**ô** order	**ü** rule	**ŦH** then	⎩ u in circus
ėr term			**zh** measure	

Gi·la monster (hē′lə), a large, poisonous lizard of the southwestern United States. It has a thick tail and a heavy body.

glide (glīd), move along smoothly, evenly, and easily: *Birds, ships, dancers, and skaters glide. verb,* **glid·ed, glid·ing.**

glove (gluv), a covering for the hand, usually with separate places for each of the four fingers and the thumb. *noun.*

goof (güf), SLANG. make a silly mistake. *verb.*

go·ril·la (gə ril′ə), the largest and strongest of the family of animals that includes monkeys and apes. It is found in the forests of central Africa. *noun.*

groove (grüv), **1** a long, narrow cut or mark often made by a tool: *My desk has a groove for pencils.* **2** any similar cut or mark: *grooves in a dirt road. noun.*

gross (grōs), **1** coarse; showing a lack of good manners: *gross manners, gross language.* **2** SLANG. an exclamation showing disgust or horror. *adjective.*

guide (gīd), person who leads you or shows the way: *We hired a guide to show us the cave. noun.*

H h

hab·it (hab′it), something you do without thinking. Doing a thing over and over again can make it a habit: *Form the habit of brushing your teeth after every meal. noun.*

han·dle (han′dl), part of a thing made to be held by the hand. Spoons, pitchers, hammers, and pails have handles. See picture. *noun.*

handles

har·bor (här′bər), a place of shelter for ships. *noun.*

heav·y (hev′ē), having much weight; large; greater than usual: *a heavy rain, a heavy crop, a heavy meal. adjective,* **heav·i·er, heav·i·est.**

herd (hėrd), group of animals of one kind, usually large animals, feeding or moving together: *a herd of cows, a herd of horses, a herd of elephants. noun.*

hey (hā), a sound made to get someone's attention, show surprise, or ask a question: *''Hey! stop!'' ''Hey? what did you say?'' interjection.*

469

hire (hīr), pay for the use of a thing or the work of a person: *She hired a car and a driver. The storekeeper hired me to deliver groceries.* verb, **hired, hir·ing.**

hiss (his), make a sound like *ss*, or like a drop of water on a hot stove. *verb.*

hob·by (hob'ē), something a person likes to do during spare time: *Our teacher's hobby is gardening.* noun, *plural* **hob·bies.**

hon·est (on'ist), fair and truthful; not lying, cheating, or stealing: *They are honest people.* *adjective.*

ho·ri·zon (hə rī'zn), line where the earth and the sky seem to meet. *You cannot see beyond the horizon.* noun.

hos·pi·tal (hos'pi təl), place for the care of the sick or of people who have been hurt. *noun.*

house·work (hous'wėrk'), work to be done in the house, such as washing, ironing, cleaning, or cooking. *noun.*

huge (hyüj), very, very large: *A whale or an elephant is a huge animal.* adjective, **hug·er, hug·est.**

hu·man-pow·ered (hyü'mən pou'ərd), getting force or energy from a person instead of from a motor; moved by the hand or foot: *A bicycle is a human-powered machine.* *adjective.*

I i

ig·nore (ig nôr'), pay no attention to: *The driver ignored the traffic light and almost hit another car.* verb, **ig·nored, ig·nor·ing.**

i·gua·na (i gwä'nə), a large lizard with a row of spikes or spines along its back. *noun.*

im·por·tant (im pôrt'nt), meaning much; having great value: *My friends are very important to me.* adjective.

in·for·ma·tion (in'fər mā'shən), things that are known; facts: *A dictionary contains much information about words.* noun.

inn (in), a place where travelers and others can get meals and a room to sleep in; a hotel: *We spent the night at a little inn.* noun.

in·spire (in spīr'), **1** fill with a thought or feeling: *A chance to try again inspired us with hope.* **2** put thought, feeling, life, or force into: *The speaker inspired the crowd. The coach inspired the team with a desire to win.* verb. **in·spired, in·spir·ing.**

i·ron (ī'ərn), a metal, from which tools and machinery are made. *Steel is made from iron.* noun.

is·land (ī'lənd), body of land surrounded by water. *See picture.* noun.

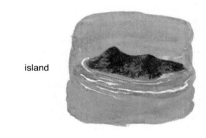

island

J j

Ja·pan (jə pan'), country made up of several islands in the Pacific, along the eastern coast of Asia. *See picture.* noun.

Japan

jew·el (jü'əl), a rare stone such as a diamond or ruby; gem. Jewels are worn in pins, rings, and other pieces of jewelry. *noun.*

K k

knob (nob), a handle on a door or drawer: *the knob on the dial of a television set. noun.*

Ko·mod·o (kə mō'dō), one of over 13,000 islands that make up the country of Indonesia, in southeastern Asia. *noun.*

L l

la·goon (lə gün'), pond or small lake near or connected with a larger body of water. *noun.*

la·pel (lə pel'), either of the two front parts of a coat folded back just below the collar. See picture. *noun.*

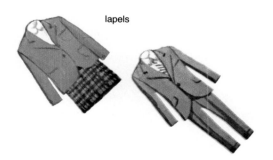
lapels

law (lô), rule made by a country or state for all the people who live there: *Everyone who lives in the United States must obey the laws. noun.*

law·yer (lô'yər), person who knows the laws and gives people advice about them. He or she also goes to court with a person to act or speak for that person. *noun.*

lens (lenz), a curved piece of glass, or something like glass, that can make things look larger or smaller. The lenses of a telescope make things look larger and nearer. *noun, plural* **lens·es.**

life preserver (pri zėr'vər), a wide belt or a jacket often made of plastic or cork, used to keep a person afloat in the water.

limb (lim), **1** leg, arm, or wing. **2** a large branch: *We tied ropes to the limb of the tree and made a swing. noun.*

lob·by (lob'ē), place in which to enter; entrance hall: *the lobby of a theater, the lobby of a hotel. noun, plural* **lob·bies.**

lodge (loj), place to live in; house, usually one to live in for a short time: *My aunt and uncle always rent a lodge in the mountains for the summer. noun.*

lung (lung), either one of a pair of organs in the chest of human beings and certain other animals that breathe air. See picture. *noun.*

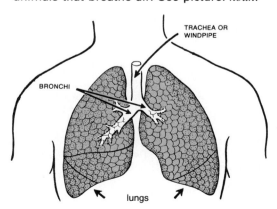
TRACHEA OR WINDPIPE
BRONCHI
lungs

471

M m

mag·a·zine (mag′ə zēn′), printed sheets of paper bound together, containing stories, news, pictures, and other items. Most magazines come out either weekly or monthly. *noun.*

ma·jor (mā′jər), **1** larger; greater: *The major part of a little baby's life is spent in sleeping.* **2** more important: *Los Angeles and Chicago are major cities. adjective.*

mam·mal (mam′əl), one of a group of warm-blooded animals with a backbone. Mammals feed their young with milk from the mother. Human beings, cattle, dogs, cats, and whales are all mammals. *noun.*

mar·ble (mär′bəl), a hard stone, white or colored. Marble is much used for statues and in buildings. *noun.*

ma·rine (mə rēn′), of the sea; found in the sea: *Seals are marine animals. adjective.*

Mars (märz), the planet nearest the earth. It is the fourth in distance from the sun and is the seventh largest of the planets. *noun.*

ma·ter·i·al (mə tir′ē əl), what a thing is made from or done with; supplies: *dress material, building materials, writing materials. noun.*

med·i·cine (med′ə sən), something to make a sick person well: *While I was sick I had to take my medicine three times a day. noun.*

met·al (met′l), material such as iron, gold, silver, and tin. *noun.*

Mex·i·co (mek′sə kō), country in North America, just south of the United States. See picture. *noun.*

mis·read (mis rēd′), read wrongly: *Sometimes I misread the sign and miss the turn. verb,* **mis·read** (mis red′), **mis·read·ing.**

mon·ster (mon′stər), in stories and movies, a make-believe, ugly-looking creature: *Did the monster in the movie frighten you? noun.*

mow (mō), **1** cut down with a machine: *mow grass. I was mowing yesterday.* **2** cut down the grass: *mow the lawn. verb,* **mowed, mowed** or **mown, mow·ing.**

my·self (mī self′), *Myself* is used instead of *me* in sentences like: *I cut myself. I helped myself to cake. pronoun, plural* **our·selves.**

N n

nar·row (nar′ō), not wide; not far from one side to the other: *a narrow piece of cloth; a narrow street. adjective.*

na·vy (nā′vē), a large group of officers and sailors and the ships on which they serve. *noun, plural* **na·vies.**

near (nir), **1** approach; come or draw close or closer to: *The train slowed down as it neared the station.* **2** close to: *Our house is near the river.* **1** *verb,* **2** *preposition.*

nine·ty (nin′tē), nine times ten; 90. *noun, plural* **nine·ties;** *adjective.*

north·east (nôrth′ēst′), **1** halfway between north and east. **2** in the northeast: *the northeast part of the country. adjective.*

no·tice (nō′tis), see; pay attention to: *I noticed a hole in my sock. verb,* **no·ticed, no·tic·ing.**

Mexico

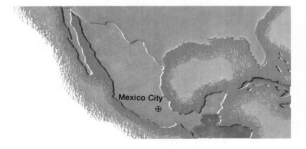

Mexico City

O o

a hat	i it	oi oil	ch child	a in about
ā age	ī ice	ou out	ng long	e in taken
ä far	o hot	u cup	sh she	ə = i in pencil
e let	ō open	u̇ put	th thin	o in lemon
ē equal	ô order	ü rule	ŦH then	u in circus
er term			zh measure	

o·bey (ō bā'), **1** do what one is told to do: *The dog obeyed and went home.* **2** follow the orders of: *You must obey the orders given to you by the police officer.* verb.

ob·sta·cle (ob'stə kəl), something that stands in the way or stops movement: *A tree fallen across the road was an obstacle to our car.* noun.

oc·to·pus (ok'tə pəs), a sea animal having a soft body and eight arms. See picture. *noun, plural* **oc·to·pus·es, oc·to·pi** (ok'tə pī).

octopus
from 6 inches (15 centimeters)
to 20 feet (6 meters) across

o·ver·all (ō'vər ôl'), **1** from one end to the other. **2** taking in everything. *adjective.*

o·ver·head (ō'vər hed'), over the head; on high; above: *the stars overhead.* adverb.

ox (oks), a kind of cattle that is fitted and trained for farm work. *noun, plural* **ox·en.**

ox·en (ok'sən), more than one ox. See picture. *noun plural.*

oxen

ox·y·gen (ok'sə jən), a gas that forms about one fifth of the air. Animals and plants cannot live without oxygen. *noun.*

o·dor (ō'dər), a smell: *The odor of roses, the odor of garbage.* noun.

of·fi·cial (ə fish'əl), person who holds a public office; an officer. *noun.*

op·e·ra·tion (op'ə rā'shən), something done to the body by a doctor using special instruments: *Taking out the tonsils is a common operation.* noun.

P p

Pa·cif·ic Ocean (pə sif'ik), the ocean west of North America and South America. It extends to Asia and Australia.

pas·sen·ger (pas'n jər), traveler in a train, bus, automobile, boat, or airplane, usually one who pays a fare. *noun.*

pat·ter (pat′ər), make rapid taps: *The rain pattered on the windowpane. verb.*

ped·al (ped′l), a lever worked by the foot: *Pushing the pedals of a bicycle makes it move. noun.*

peer (pir), look closely to see clearly. See picture. *verb.*

peer—a girl peering at goldfish

pi·o·neer (pī′ə nir′), person who settles in a part of a country where very few people have lived before. *noun.*

pi·rate (pī′rit), person who robs ships; robber on the sea. *noun.*

plan·et (plan′it), one of the heavenly bodies that move around the sun. Mercury, Venus, the earth, Mars, Jupiter, Saturn, Uranus, Neptune, and Pluto are planets. *noun.*

plunge (plunj), throw oneself into water, danger, or a fight: *She plunged into the lake to save the drowning swimmer. verb,* **plunged, plung·ing.**

poi·son (poi′zn), a substance that is very dangerous to life and health. *noun.*

polar bear (pō′lər), a large white bear of the arctic regions. See picture.

por·tion (pôr′shən), part or share: *We study math for a portion of each school day. noun.*

prair·ie (prer′ē), a large area of level or rolling land with grass but few or no trees. *noun.*

praise (prāz), **1** say that a thing or person is good. **2** speak well of: *The coach praised the team for its fine playing. verb,* **praised, prais·ing.**

pro·gram (prō′gram), a broadcast on radio or television: *a news program. noun.*

Q q

quar·ter (kwôr′tər), **1** one of four equal parts; half of a half; one fourth. **2** coin of the United States and Canada equal to 25 cents. Four quarters make one dollar. *noun.*

polar bear
about 4 feet (1 meter) high
at the shoulder and
about 8 feet (2½ meters) long

R r

a hat	**i** it	**oi** oil	**ch** child		a in about
ā age	**ī** ice	**ou** out	**ng** long		e in taken
ä far	**o** hot	**u** cup	**sh** she	**ə** =	i in pencil
e let	**ō** open	**u̇** put	**th** thin		o in lemon
ē equal	**ô** order	**ü** rule	**ℾH** then		u in circus
ėr term			**zh** measure		

rail·ing (rā′ling), **1** fence made of rails. **2** rail used as a guard or support on a stairway, platform, or bridge: *Hang on to the railing.* *noun.*

rare (rer *or* rar), hardly ever seen or found. *adjective,* **rar·er, rar·est.**

res·taur·ant (res′tər ənt), place to buy and eat a meal. *noun.*

rink (ringk), **1** sheet of ice for skating. **2** a smooth floor for roller-skating. See picture. *noun.*

rink—a hockey rink

ro·bot (rō′bət *or* rō′bot), machine that acts and works like a human being. See picture. *noun.*

row (rō), use oars to move a boat through the water: *Row to the island. verb.*

S s

safe·ty (sāf′tē), a state of being free from harm or danger or accident: *Safety is very important to everyone. noun.*

sa·la·mi (sə lä′mē), a kind of thick sausage. It is usually sliced and eaten cold. *noun,* *plural* **sa·la·mis.**

robot—robot pushing a child

475

saucer|squid

sau·cer (sô'sər), **1** a shallow dish to set a cup on. **2** something round and shallow like a saucer. *noun.*

sau·cer·like (sô'sər līk'), shaped like a shallow dish or a saucer. *adjective.*

scale (skāl), one of the thin, flat, hard plates forming the outside covering of some fishes, snakes, and lizards. *noun.*

scal·y (skā'lē), covered with scales; having scales like a fish, a snake, or a lizard. *adjective,* **scal·i·er, scal·i·est.**

scarf (skärf), a long, broad strip of silk, lace, or other material, worn about the neck, shoulders, or head. See picture. *noun, plural* **scarfs, scarves** (skärvz).

scarf

sci·ence (sī'əns), a careful study of facts about the earth or anything on it. There are many different kinds of science. *noun.*

sci·en·tist (sī'ən tist), a person who studies a science. There are many different kinds of scientists. *noun.*

sculp·tor (skulp'tər), person who carves or models figures. Sculptors make statues of marble and bronze. *noun.*

sculp·ture (skulp'chər), a statue or figure made from stone or other material: *There are many pieces of sculpture in the museum. noun.*

ser·i·ous (sir'ē əs), in earnest; not fooling: *Are you joking or serious? adjective.*

sher·iff (sher'if), the most important law officer of a county. *noun.*

sigh (sī), let out a very long, deep breath: *We heard her sigh. verb.*

skid (skid), slip or slide sideways while moving: *The car skidded on the slippery road. verb,* **skid·ded, skid·ding.**

slick (slik), slippery; greasy: *a road slick with ice or mud. adjective.*

sod (sod), piece or layer of ground that contains the grass and its roots. *noun.*

so·fa (sō'fə), a long seat or couch having a back and arms. *noun.*

sol·id (sol'id), **1** not liquid: *Water becomes solid when it freezes.* **2** hard; firm: *solid rock. adjective.*

some·day (sum'dā), at some time in the future. *adverb.*

some·place (sum'plās), in or to some place; somewhere. *adverb.*

speech (spēch), **1** spoken words. **2 part of speech,** any of the groups into which words are divided. Nouns, verbs, adjectives and adverbs are all parts of speech. *noun, plural* **speech·es.**

splint (splint), a kind of brace made of wood, metal, or plaster that is used to hold a broken bone in place. *noun.*

sprain (sprān), twist a joint or muscle: *I sprained my ankle. verb.*

square (skwer *or* skwar), **1** figure with four equal sides and four equal corners (□). **2** having this shape: *a square box. This table is square.* **1** *noun,* **2** *adjective,* **squar·er, squar·est.**

squid (skwid), a sea animal like an octopus but having ten arms instead of eight. See picture. *noun, plural* **squids** *or* **squid.**

squid
this type up to 8 feet
(2½ meters) long with arms

stat·ue (stach′ü), model of a person or animal carved in stone or made from other materials. See picture. *noun.*

statue

tel·e·scope (tel′ə skōp), an instrument for making objects that are far away seem to be nearer and larger. The stars are studied by means of telescopes. See picture. *noun.*

telescope

stream·lined (strēm′līnd′), having a shape that makes it easy to pass through air or water. The fastest cars, airplanes, and boats have streamlined bodies. See picture. *adjective.*

streamlined

tell·tale (tel′tāl′), **1** person who tells tales on others. **2** serving as a sign or as a clue to something: *a telltale fingerprint.* **1** *noun,* **2** *adjective.*

ten·nis (ten′is), game played by two or four players on a special court, in which a ball is hit with a racket over a net. See picture. *noun.*

tennis—two players playing tennis

sur·face (sėr′fis), any side, face, or upper part of something; the outside: *The surface of the road is rough. The lake had a smooth surface. noun.*

sur·vive (sər vīv′), continue to live; continue to be: *Only ten of the ship's crew survived the shipwreck. verb,* **sur·vived, sur·viv·ing.**

ter·ri·ble (ter′ə bəl), causing great fear; awful: *The terrible storm destroyed many homes. adjective.*

thir·ty (thėr′tē) three times ten; 30. *noun, plural* **thir·ties;** *adjective.*

tomb (tüm), grave or vault for a dead body, often above ground. *noun.*

tool (tül), hammer, saw, shovel, or anything else used in doing work: *Plumbers and carpenters need tools. noun.*

T t

taps (taps), signal on a bugle to put out lights at night. Taps are also sounded when a person who dies in the armed forces is buried. *noun plural.*

train·ing (trā′ning), education in some art or trade: *training for teachers. noun.*

tramp (tramp), **1** walk heavily: *They tramped across the floor in their heavy boots.* **2** walk; go on foot: *The young hikers tramped through the mountains. verb.*

treas·ure (trezh′ər), something much loved or of great value: *He kept his treasures in a safe place. noun.*

tune (tün *or* tyün), **1** piece of music: *He played a tune on the violin.* **2** the proper pitch: *The piano is out of tune. Please sing in tune.* **3** put in tune: *We should have the piano tuned.* 1, 2 *noun,* 3 *verb,* **tuned, tun·ing.**

U u

un·plug (un plug′), pull out the plug from an electric outlet. *verb,* **un·plugged, un·plug·ging.**

un·sink·a·ble (un singk′ə bəl), not able to be sunk; built to stay above water. *adjective.*

V v

vac·uum cleaner (vak′yü əm *or* vak′yüm), machine for cleaning carpets or floors. See picture.

vacuum cleaner

ve·hi·cle (vē′ə kəl), something people can ride in or on. Automobiles, bicycles, boats, and planes are vehicles. *noun.*

vel·vet (vel′vit), a kind of thick, soft cloth. It may be made of silk, rayon, or cotton. *noun.*

W w

wade (wād), walk through water, snow, sand, mud, or anything that makes walking hard: *He waded across the river. verb,* **wad·ed, wad·ing.**

waist (wāst), the part of the body between the ribs and the hips. *noun.*

wai·tress (wā′tris), woman who waits on tables in a restaurant. *noun, plural* **wai·tress·es.**

wal·let (wol′it), a small, flat case for carrying money or cards in one's pocket or handbag; billfold. *noun.*

waste (wāst), make poor use of: *Though they had much work to do, they wasted their time doing nothing. verb,* **wast·ed, wast·ing.**

weath·er (weᴛʜ′ər), the state of the air around and above a certain place: *The weather is cold and rainy here today. noun.*

weld (weld), **1** join pieces of metal together by making the parts that touch so hot that they melt, flow together, and become one piece in cooling. **2** unite closely: *Working together welded them into a team. verb.*

wil·low (wil′ō), kind of tree or bush with long, thin branches and narrow leaves. The branches of most willows bend easily. *noun.*

writ·er (rī′tər), author; person who makes up stories, books, poems, or the like. *noun.*

Z z

zoom (züm), move suddenly and rapidly: *The car zoomed past us. verb.*

Page 144: From "Musically: Patrice Rushen" by Ohaji Abdallah. Text copyright © 1981 by Johnson Publishing Company, Inc. Reprinted by permission of EBONY JR!
Page 166: From *Trouble for Lucy* by Carla Stevens. Copyright © 1979 by Carla Stevens. Reprinted by permission of Tichnor & Fields/Clarion Books, a Houghton Mifflin Company.
Page 221: Abridged and adapted from *Wild Animals, Gentle Women,* copyright © 1978 by Margery Facklam. Reprinted by permission of Harcourt Brace Jovanovich, Inc.
Page 226: Adaptation of *The Deep Dives of Stanley Whale* (text only) by Nathaniel Benchley. Copyright © 1973 by Nathaniel Benchley. Reprinted by permission of Harper & Row, Publishers, Inc.
Page 244: Adapted by permission of Four Winds Press, a division of Scholastic Inc. from *The Week Mom Unplugged the TVs* by Terry Phelan. Copyright © 1979 by Terry Phelan.
Page 256: Adapted with permission of Macmillan Publishing Company from *Gila Monsters Meet You at the Airport* by Marjorie Weinman Sharmat. Copyright © 1980 Marjorie Weinman Sharmat.
Page 273: "Miracle in Rome" adapted by permission of Random House, Inc. from *Wonder Women of Sports* by Betty Millsaps Jones. Copyright © 1981 by Random House, Inc.
Page 333: From "Truly My Own" by Vanessa Howard. From *The Voice of the Children* collected by June Jordan and Terri Bush. Copyright © 1968, 1969, 1970 by The Voice of the Children, Inc. Reprinted by permission of Holt, Rinehart and Winston, Publishers and Julian Bach Literary Agency, Inc.
Page 336: From "A Life on Ice" by Shirley Lee, *Boys' Life,* January 1983. Reprinted by permission of the author.
Page 342: *A Chair for My Mother* (text only) by Vera B. Williams. Copyright © 1982 by Vera B. Williams. Adapted by permission of Greenwillow Books (A Division of William Morrow & Company).
Page 379: From "Limericks" as it appeared in *Speak Up!* by David McCord. Copyright © 1979 by David McCord. By permission of Little, Brown and Company.
Page 385: From "What a Place for Fossils" by Merrill and Jennifer Horenstein as told to Sallie Luther. Copyright © 1981 National Wildlife Federation. Adapted from the January 1981 issue of *Ranger Rick* magazine, with permission of the publisher, the National Wildlife Federation.
Page 396: From *Cyrus, the Unsinkable Sea Serpent* by Bill Peet. Copyright © 1975 by William B. Peet. Reprinted by permission of Houghton Mifflin Company and Andre Deutsch.
Page 410: From "Dragons of the Sea" by Bill Keenan. Copyright © 1981 National Wildlife Federation. Adapted from the December 1981 issue of *Ranger Rick* magazine, with permission of the publisher, the National Wildlife Federation.
Page 430: "Your Computer, Your Dog, and You" from Beginners' Corner by Matthew Yuen, *Softalk Magazine,* April 1983. Copyright © 1983 Softalk Publishing, Inc. Adapted by permission.
Page 435: "Such a Nice Little Planet" by Suzan Jarvis. Copyright © 1981 by Suzan Jarvis. First appeared in *Cricket,* March 1981. Adapted by permission of the author.
Page 453: Adapted from *The Robot Birthday* by Eve Bunting. Copyright © 1980 by Eve Bunting. Reprinted by permission of the publisher, E. P. Dutton, Inc.

Cover Artist
Mark Stearney

Photographs
Page 25: Red hind fish—Fred Bavendam/Peter Arnold, Inc.; Horseshoe crab—Ronald F. Thomas/BRUCE COLEMAN INC.; Alligator—Joseph Van Wormer/BRUCE COLEMAN INC.; Ants—Hans Pfletschinger/Peter Arnold, Inc.; Ants in Amber—Edward S. Ross; Alligator fossil—Norman Owen Tomalin/BRUCE COLEMAN INC.; Horseshoe crab fossil—Courtesy, Field Museum of Natural History, Chicago; Carbonized fish fossil—George Roos/Peter Arnold, Inc.; Page 26: Tiger—E. R. Degginger; Eagle—Stephen J. Krasemann/DRK PHOTO; Page 27: Orangutans—Wolfgang Bayer Productions; Polar bear—E. R. Degginger; Pages 38–39: Flip & Debra Schulke/Black Star; Page 40: Workers in zoo—Michael Goss for Scott, Foresman; Zookeeper— James P. Rowan; Page 41: Michael Goss for Scott, Foresman; Pages 46–48: Babe gets her tooth pulled—© *Chicago Tribune.* Photos by Jerry Tomaselli; Pages 98–100: © 1983 Yiorgos Naoum/ Photojournalist; Page 114: *The Boston Globe;* Page 139: South Street, N. Y.—Photo by Donna Svennevik. Project of the Public Art Fund, Inc.; Zipper and Tunnel—From *Street Murals* by Volker Barthelmeh © 1982 Alfred A. Knopf, Inc.; Page 142: Sirenz—Robert B. Tolchin for Scott, Foresman; Page 145: B/W photo by Bobby Holland. Courtesy Elektra-Asylum Records; Page 146: 146 (t): Engraving by J. Pass from ENCYCLOPEDIA LONDINENSIS, 1818/Courtesy of The Art Institute of Chicago; 147 (r): Courtesy United States Naval Academy Museum; Page 156: Deborah Butterfield— Linda Best; Sculpture "Ponder"—Jamey Schlepp; Pages 174–175: Mary M. Tremaine/Root Resources; Page 178: Solomon D. Butcher Collection/Nebraska State Historical Society; Page 180: Drawn by Paul Frenzeny & Jules Tavernier. From *Harper's Weekly,* 1874; Page 181: Solomon D. Butcher Collection/Nebraska State Historical Society; Page 186: Los Angeles County Museum of Natural History; Page 187: Courtesy California State Library; Pages 200–201: James M. Cribb/Subtidal Photography; Page 212: Killer Whale—K. C. Balcomb/MOCLIPS CETOLOGICAL SOCIETY; Beluga Whale—E. R. Degginger/BRUCE COLEMAN INC.; Page 213: Humpback whale—Ed Robinson/Tom Stack & Associates; Dolphin—C. Allan Morgan; Page 222: Beluga whale—© Robert Rattner 1982; Page 223: Courtesy Margery Facklam; Page 225: Bob Moreland; Page 235: Squid—David C. Haas/Tom Stack & Associates; Pages 271–272: Pepe Trevino (3 photos)—George H. Harrison; Page 275: Wide World Photos; Pages 280–281: Earl Dibble/FPG; Page 285: © Norman Prince; Page 286: From AMONG THE MAYA RUINS by Ann & Myra Sutton. Photo/Matilda Metcalf; Page 289: Courtesy Mexican National Tourist Council; Page 303: Bohdan Hrynewych/Southern Light; Pages 320–321: Ric Helstrom/Tom Stack & Associates; Page 322: Courtesy State of California, Dept. of Parks & Recreation; Pages 337–340: Chuck O'Rear; Pages 356–357: Clyde H. Smith/FPG; Page 366: Toad—Edward S. Ross; Fawn—Bob & Ira Spring/FPG; Arctic hare— Stephen J. Krasemann/Peter Arnold, Inc.; Page 367: Walking